W9-AZX-855

SAVE-IT-FORWARD
SUPPERS

SAVE-IT-FORWARD
SUPPERS

A SIMPLE STRATEGY TO SAVE
TIME, MONEY, AND SANITY

CYNDI KANE

Illustrations by
JEANNINE BULLEIGH

WILLIAM MORROW
An Imprint of HarperCollins Publishers

The best way to acquire true dignity is to
wash one's own clothes and boil one's own pot.

—ST. FRANCIS XAVIER

To my saintly family,
who has endured a lifetime of
culinary experiments

Contents

Foreword

I have a declaration to make: My dear friend Cyndi, whom I nicknamed "Hyacinth" more than twenty years ago, is a better cook than I. Now, lest you think I'm being self-deprecating and/or overly complimentary due to the fact that I'm writing the foreword to my best buddy's cookbook: I promise that neither is true! Yes, I may have a cooking show on TV and a few cookbooks under my belt, but my simple truth is that if there's one home cook I most aspire to be like, it's definitely Hyacinth!

The two of us go way back—and I mean way, way back. Our husbands' families have known each other for five generations if you count our children, and because my in-laws were close friends with hers, Hyacinth became one of my very first friends when I married Ladd and moved to our small town of Pawhuska. She and I didn't have to love each other, but we hit it off from day one, and we've had many memorable and formative experiences together—including being present at a couple of our kids' births. (Now that's love right there!)

As a friend of Hy's for so many years, I've gotten to witness her steady approach to domestic bliss—specifically, her approach to cooking. I find myself continually in awe of her ability to combine flavor, creativity, and interest with day-in/day-out frugality and resourcefulness. Where I have

always flown by the seat of my pants in the kitchen, grabbing whatever ingredients sound good and giving nary a thought to tomorrow, Hyacinth has always taken a deliciously thoughtful, more methodical approach. Yes, she plans her meals ahead of time—but not just that. As you'll see in this cookbook, she also makes plans for the leftovers, considering them springboards for even more cooking. Somehow in the process of making dinner daily for her family for almost thirty years, she developed a rhythm and a feel for which meal elements would likely be left after one meal . . . and her mind churned with ideas for what they could become tomorrow, or the day after that, or the day after that. And that's what *Save-It-Forward Suppers* is all about!

Another important gift Hyacinth has, in addition to her everyday practicality, is that she doesn't do well with the mundane. She doesn't like to be bored. So within the confines (she will laugh at that word) of being the cook of her family in a small town in middle America, she never has let herself slip into all the predictable dishes and all the safe, palatable ingredients. Amid the comforting and familiar soups and casseroles, Hy isn't afraid to whip out a gorgeous shakshuka or jambalaya just to keep things exciting. The variety of recipes in these pages is a delight, and a reflection of Hy herself.

Hyacinth is no ordinary cook, and this cookbook is probably unlike any you've seen before. From her cheeky writing (which always cracks me up) to the charming recipe illustrations to the clever weekly menus that fit together like some kind of scrumptious puzzle, you'll surely be inspired to tackle dinnertime in a fresh, fun, and purposeful way—and approach your cooking life with brand-new excitement.

And knowing what I know about my friend Hyacinth, nothing would make her happier than that.

—Ree

Introduction

Recently I had one of those unexpected blessings of motherhood, one that I could not have envisioned as I was slogging away in the gritty (but joyous!) muck of raising young kids. My daughter, newly married and budget-minded, was preparing lunches for her upcoming work week. It was hard for me to believe that the kid who had stood on a chair next to me stirring muffin batter was now the one bustling about in her own kitchen. But then she stumped me with a simple question. "Mom," she asked, "do you like to cook?"

I was flummoxed. *Hmm . . . do I like to cook? Do I? Like it?* I finally concluded that the answer was "not really," which shocked me a bit. As a homeschool mom of four who has religiously cooked three meals a day for decades now, I would have thought I could have managed a "By golly, I do, dear!"

I think I could have managed a yes if I had felt like a pro in the kitchen. Though my food is tasty, my kitchen is always a mess by the time I've cooked a meal, and my Fitbit registers like I've run a marathon.

However, here's what I do like: the payoff. It is more than just the pleasure of eating yummy food. It is the joy found in providing the countless meals that have prompted

my family to gather around the table to share a moment in our day. And around that table, a life has been built. A life that my daughter now wants to emulate. Wow, that's beyond gratifying . . . I find myself a little teary as I write this. I didn't know precisely what the result would be; I just knew that as a young mama, I had read that kids who had regular dinners with the family were happier, healthier, and more successful. I adopted meal prep as a sacred obligation, not allowing myself to think about whether I liked it or not. I just knew that I wanted that life for my kids.

But that commitment didn't change the fact that I wasn't terribly dexterous or efficient at cooking. I did have one advantage, though, as I was trying to get my family fed: my mother was a child of the Depression, and her mother was a widow with four kids to feed. My mother learned resourcefulness when stretching meals, and mercifully, I inherited this ability. This book is the culmination of watching my mom effortlessly create inventive meal plans, combined with my own modern spin on feeding my family for more than three decades (*yikes*—where have the years gone?!).

WHAT DO I MEAN BY "SAVE IT FORWARD"?

It's exhausting to cook an entire meal from the ground up every night. Stop that! I have a better way—an efficient method of creating healthy, tasty family meals even if cooking is not your thing. For this book I've created fifteen separate weeks of meals in which every time you cook a dish, you'll be saving ingredients forward—that is, preparing some of the components in a way that will let you use them to make an entirely different meal later in that week. I don't know about you, but my family is not overly excited about warmed-up leftovers, and this method reimagines the components in ways that never seem like last night's

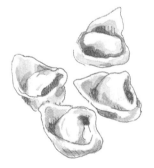

rehashed seconds. But, if thinking about an entire week of meals sounds too ambitious for you, no problem—each recipe can stand alone! That said, I hope I can persuade you to try my method, even if it might seem tricky at first. I'll be with you every step of the way!

Though this book contains more than one hundred forty recipes in this book, it's really more of a method—or a mindset, to be more precise. I've tried to think of the various moods and situations a family might encounter and provide a weekly game plan: summer grilling, winter comfort foods, pantry items, shortcuts, belt-tightening—*I've got you!* Your family will have its own quirks, but I believe that this save-it-forward method will give you some tools in your culinary toolbox to help solve your unique mealtime problems.

Here are my goals for feeding my family. Are you my culinary soulmate? Hope so!

1. **Delicious**—well, of course! (Though some days, I'm just shooting for getting people fed.)
2. **Kid-friendly but adventuresome.** My adult kids eat just about everything. When they were smaller, I didn't insist that they clean their plates when I served them something new, but I asked them to try it. I purposefully cooked a variety of cuisines in order to broaden their palates. I will admit, though, that when I knew a dish would be a little weird for them, I'd try to make sure there was something in the meal that I knew they liked, like buttered bread or fruit.
3. **Healthy.** I'm not the kind of gal who throws chia seeds into everything, but I slip in veggies when I can and keep simple carbs to a minimum throughout the week. My husband is a gluten-free guy, so I generally cook something that is either GF or can be made so with

an easy modification. I'm often following one plan or another to lose a few pounds, so most of the meals can be modified to suit my current dietary shenanigans.

4. **Budget-friendly.** As I mentioned, my mother was a child in the Depression, and that mindset is in our family DNA. In other words, I'm a cheapskate! I am conscious of our food budget, and if an ingredient is expensive, I stretch it with less costly components in that meal or later in the week.

I am hopeful that this book will make your family deliriously happy, and that you'll be building family memories as you gather around the table—with less stress and effort on your part. Let's do this thing!

Love,
Cyndi

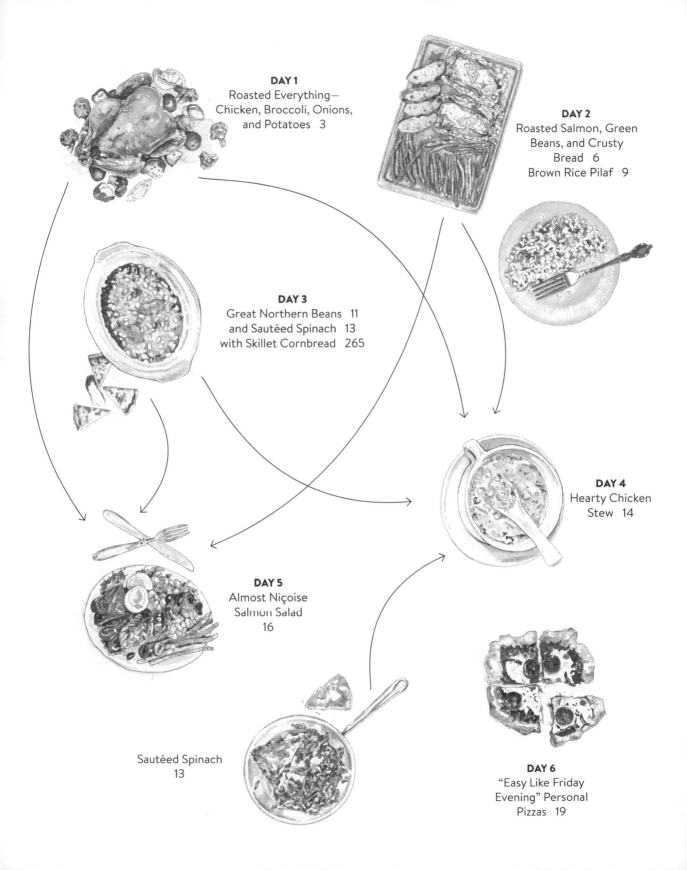

DAY 1
Roasted Everything—
Chicken, Broccoli, Onions,
and Potatoes 3

DAY 2
Roasted Salmon, Green
Beans, and Crusty
Bread 6
Brown Rice Pilaf 9

DAY 3
Great Northern Beans 11
and Sautéed Spinach 13
with Skillet Cornbread 265

DAY 4
Hearty Chicken
Stew 14

DAY 5
Almost Niçoise
Salmon Salad
16

Sautéed Spinach
13

DAY 6
"Easy Like Friday
Evening" Personal
Pizzas 19

Simple Meats and Veggies Week

Since you might be new to this save-it-forward way of thinking about meal prep, I want to keep this first week very streamlined and straightforward. Each day, you'll either be saving forward components for another meal or, even better, you'll be enjoying a meal in which you have nothing to cook because all the components have been saved forward.

For a gentle introduction to the method, we're starting with a week of simple meats and veggies, but don't worry—you didn't sign up for a monk's life when you bought this book! These meals are flavorful, economical, and healthful, and you'll even get to reward yourself with a pizza at the end of the week because you've eaten so darn virtuously all week long.

ROASTED EVERYTHING—CHICKEN, BROCCOLI, ONIONS, AND POTATOES

Olive oil, for rubbing

1 tablespoon spice rub of your choice: a combination of garlic and onion powder, seasoning blends, paprika, cayenne pepper, and so on

2 teaspoons table salt, plus more to taste

1 teaspoon ground black pepper, plus more to taste

One 5- to 6-pound chicken (or larger or smaller, depending on your family size; a **SAVE-IT-FORWARD** item)

1 lemon, cut lengthwise into 6 wedges

3 medium yellow onions, 2 cut lengthwise into wedges (a **SAVE-IT-FORWARD** item)

2 to 3 pounds potatoes, peeled (if thick-skinned) and cut into 1½-inch cubes (a **SAVE-IT-FORWARD** item)

2 medium bunches broccoli (about 2 pounds), cut into 1-inch florets

Special tool: extra-wide foil (optional)

Is it strange for me to say that I'm not crazy about the opening recipe in my cookbook? Here's the deal: I'm just not a gal who craves a big hunk of meat; I prefer it as a lesser player in a meal starring grains and veggies. The carnivores in my family, however, violently disagree with me, choosing meals that a caveman would relish. So, it's a dance—the yin and yang of cooking for a family.

1. The chicken will be placed on a lower oven rack and the veggies will be on a higher rack, so adjust your racks accordingly. Preheat the oven to 450°F. Cover two sheet pans with foil to make cleanup easier (extra-wide foil is helpful!).

2. I consider preparing chicken a straight-up biohazard situation, so I take several steps in advance so everything is in place before I get started. Chefs call this *mise en place*, and this is the perfect time to take a tip from the pros. Pour a bit of olive oil in a small bowl. Mix the spice rub, salt, and pepper in another small bowl. You don't want to touch your spice jars with your radioactive chicken hands.

3. Remove all the icky stuff from inside the chicken—you know, that bag of *who knows what that is*. I discard it because I don't want to think about it anymore, but I bet some of you are less squeamish and cheerily repurpose it. I applaud you! In the old days, we were told to rinse chicken, but that's not the new protocol because it drips biohazard liquid everywhere.

4. Dry the chicken thoroughly with paper towels. Carefully separate the skin from the breasts (which will ensure a crispy, pretty skin), rub the chicken with oil, and cover it with the spice rub.

5. Place all the lemon wedges and half an onion, in wedges, in the chicken cavity.

6. Place the chicken on a wire rack (if you have one) in the middle of one of the sheet pans, breast side up, and set the pan on the lower oven rack.

7. Roast the chicken for 15 minutes to create a crispy, pretty skin, then lower the oven heat to 375°F and roast for about 15 minutes per pound. To test the doneness, if you have an instant-read thermometer, insert it at the inner thigh, not touching the bone, and it should read at least 165°F. I generally can't find my thermometer, so I just see if the juices run clear in the thigh area.

8. While the chicken is roasting, toss the potatoes, broccoli, and remaining onion wedges separately with a bit of olive oil to coat lightly, then season with salt and pepper. Add the potatoes on one side of the second sheet pan, the broccoli in the middle, and the onion at the other end so you can remove one vegetable at a time if they cook at different rates.

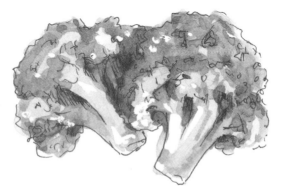

TO DO TONIGHT:
Place the chicken carcass and skin right into the crock of a slow cooker for Overnight Chicken Broth (page 268). You'll be using 12 cups of broth this week, and this recipe will make at least that much. With just a little effort, you'll save enough money for a couple of trips to Starbucks!

9. Stick the veggies in the oven on the higher rack to roast. Check them for doneness after 30 minutes and roast longer, if necessary. When each veggie is cooked to your perfection, perhaps at different rates, remove it to a serving platter. Personally, I like mine very browned—particularly the broccoli!

10. When the chicken is done, give it a 10-minute rest, if you can shoo your family away. In terms of carving your chicken, my recommendation is to let everyone snag their favorite part, whether that's the breast, drumstick, thigh—whatever! Though you will save forward the remainder of the chicken, various bits and pieces will be fine for that purpose, so let your family have what they want tonight.

SAVE IT FORWARD—CHICKEN: After your family demolishes the chicken, finish the demolition by removing the rest of the chicken from the bone, placing it in a container, and refrigerating it. (Use the bones and skin in the stock tonight; see **To Do Tonight**). You'll need 1 to 2 cups of chicken for Hearty Chicken Stew (page 14) later in the week. If there are additional leftovers, they can be used for chicken fried rice (see **Lunch Bits and Bobs**, page 10).

SAVE IT FORWARD—POTATOES: If you have leftover potatoes, add them to Almost Niçoise Salmon Salad (page 16) later in the week.

SAVE-IT-FORWARD—ONION: While you are chopping onions, chop one for tomorrow's Brown Rice Pilaf (page 9). No need to shed tears two days in a row!

ROASTED SALMON, GREEN BEANS, AND CRUSTY BREAD

The simplest of meals, and best of all, the leftovers will become a delightful salad later in the week. Serve with Brown Rice Pilaf (page 9).

1 large loaf crusty French bread, cut into 1-inch slices

1½ cups mayonnaise

½ cup olive oil

3 garlic cloves, minced

Zest and juice of 1 lemon

1 teaspoon table salt

½ teaspoon ground black pepper

2 pounds green beans

2 to 3 pounds fresh salmon fillets, thawed, if frozen (I like wild-caught salmon)

1½ teaspoons Dijon or whole-grain mustard (or regular mustard, if it's all you have!)

½ teaspoon paprika

½ teaspoon dried dill, or 1½ teaspoons minced fresh dill (optional)

1. Arrange two oven racks: an upper one for the bread and salmon and a lower one for the green beans. Preheat the oven to 400°F. Cover two sheet pans with foil for easy cleanup.

2. Place the bread slices on one of the sheet pans and toast on the upper rack for 5 minutes, until lightly browned. Remove from the pan.

3. In a medium bowl, make a sauce: whisk the mayonnaise, olive oil, garlic, lemon zest and juice, salt, and pepper. Slather the toasted bread with a thin (or thick!) layer of the sauce, but be sure to reserve 1½ cups for the beans and salmon. Set aside.

4. Place the green beans on the second sheet pan, toss lightly with ¾ cup of the remaining sauce, spread them out evenly, and roast on the lower rack for 25 to 30 minutes, or until cooked to your liking (but don't be afraid to let them become very browned and flavorful!).

5. Meanwhile, place the salmon on a large sheet of foil. Whisk the Dijon, paprika, and dill (if using) into the remaining ¾ cup sauce and spread it evenly over each fillet. Wrap the foil edges over the salmon to form a packet and enclose all the fillets; the goal is to keep in all the juices.

6. Place the salmon packet on the first sheet pan and place it on the rack above the beans. The salmon will take 15 to

TO DO TONIGHT:
Start soaking the Great Northern beans for Day 3 (see page 12). Place them in a slow cooker, add water to cover by about 3 inches, and let sit overnight (don't turn the slow cooker on).

18 minutes to get to 120°F. The USDA recommends that it register 145°F, but the salmon will continue to cook a bit in the packet after you remove it from the oven. In my opinion, 145°F seems a bit overcooked. I remove mine from the oven when the fillets have barely lost their translucency.

7. After the salmon has been in the oven for 10 minutes, place the toasts on the sheet pan next to the salmon. Toast until very brown, 8 to 10 minutes. Serve alongside the green beans and the salmon.

SAVE IT FORWARD—SALMON AND GREEN BEANS: Save any remaining salmon and green beans for Almost Niçoise Salmon Salad (page 16). The quantity of leftovers can vary, and there are plenty of other goodies on the salad, so you need not worry about a precise amount of leftovers.

BROWN RICE PILAF

2 tablespoons olive oil

2 tablespoons butter

1 medium yellow onion, chopped (approximately 1 cup), saved forward

2 garlic cloves, minced (jarred garlic is fine!)

2 cups uncooked long-grain brown rice

4 cups (1 quart) Overnight Chicken Broth (page 268) or other chicken broth

1½ teaspoons table salt, plus more to taste

1 teaspoon ground black pepper, plus more to taste

1½ cups corn kernels (fresh from the cob if you are fancy, frozen if you are me, or even canned!)

Brown (versus white) rice might be the one healthier option I'm innately attracted to. Aside from the benefit of not spiking your blood sugar as white rice does, its chewy texture is just more interesting. It does take longer to cook than white rice, so get this started as your first action item when preparing your meal. Or heck, use white rice if you want to! Just reduce your cooking time accordingly.

1. Heat the oil and butter in a large saucepan over medium-high heat. Add the onion and sauté for 3 to 5 minutes, until softened; add the garlic and cook for 1 or 2 minutes, until fragrant. Add the rice and stir to coat with the oil and butter. Add the broth, salt, and pepper and bring to a boil. Cover and reduce the heat to low.

2. Simmer until the rice is tender and the liquid is absorbed, around 45 minutes. Keep the lid on during the cooking, but check the rice for doneness after 35 to 40 minutes. If it is not yet tender and the water has been absorbed, add ¼ cup hot water, stir, and continue cooking. Add more hot water as needed until the cooking is complete.

3. Turn off the heat, add the corn to the cooked rice, and let the residual heat warm it through. (If you are using fresh from the cob, add it when there is still a little liquid in the pan, when the rice has cooked for 35 minutes or so.)

4. Fluff the rice, taste, and add more salt and pepper as desired.

SAVE IT FORWARD—BROWN RICE PILAF: Save 1½ cups for Hearty Chicken Stew (page 14) later in the week.

LUNCH BITS AND BOBS: *Make a quick chicken fried rice from the leftover Brown Rice Pilaf, chicken, and roasted veggies. Heat 1 or 2 tablespoons vegetable oil, add the rice, and sauté until it starts to brown a bit. Add the chicken and veggies and cook until warmed, stirring occasionally. Make an open space in the middle of the rice mixture and crack an egg into it and scramble it. Incorporate the scrambled egg into the rice mixture and give it a splash of soy sauce, to taste.*

GREAT NORTHERN BEANS

2 pounds dried Great Northern beans, soaked overnight (see page 8; a **SAVE-IT-FORWARD** item)

1 ham hock (see Note on page 12)

2 tablespoons chicken or ham base/concentrate or 1 packet Goya ham concentrate

2 bay leaves

2 teaspoons onion powder

2 teaspoons garlic powder

2 celery stalks, sliced thin

Dash of cayenne pepper (optional, if you like a bit of heat)

1 teaspoon table salt, plus more to taste

1 teaspoon ground black pepper, plus more to taste

½ of a ham steak (¾ to 1 pound), cut into 1-inch dice, half reserved as a **SAVE-IT-FORWARD** item (optional)

There is something so elemental about a pot of beans. It may not seem that exciting, but don't skip it—beans are nourishing and economical, hearty and homey. Paired with a side of greens and a piece of buttery cornbread, they are one of life's simplest pleasures.

Ham hocks will pack a punch of meaty flavor for little money, but my guys like actual chunks of meat in their bean bowls, so I buy one of those thick, vacuum-packed ham steaks. If you like to eat less meat or are on a strict budget, you can skip it and still have a lovely meal.

You'll be saving forward your leftovers for two more meals this week, so don't fret about cooking two pounds of beans. Serve with Skillet Cornbread (page 265)—delicious!

NOTE ON HAM HOCKS: You can buy these fresh or frozen, and they generally come in a pack of two or three. I always individually wrap, package, and freeze the extras since they are so handy to have in the freezer for a pot of beans. When cooking with ham hocks, you can take the ham meat off the bone at the end of the cooking period and return it to the pot.

1. Drain the water from the soaked beans and remove any funky-looking beans or rocks. Return the beans to the slow cooker and add fresh water to cover the beans by 1 or 2 inches. Add the ham hock, chicken or ham base, bay leaves, onion powder, garlic powder, celery, cayenne (if using), salt, and pepper.

2. Most newfangled slow cookers will thoroughly cook soaked beans in 4 to 6 hours on low or 2 to 4 hours on high. I apparently need a new slow cooker, because it took my old geezer 8 hours on low to cook these until tender. Bottom line: your mileage may vary if you have an older model. If at any time you think they are taking too long on low, just switch it over to a higher setting for a while.

3. If you are using the ham steak, add it to the slow cooker about 15 minutes before serving to heat it through. Remove the ham hock before serving. Feel free to remove the meat from the bone and add it back to the beans. Adjust the seasoning with salt and pepper and discard the bay leaves.

SAVE IT FORWARD—BEANS: Refrigerate the extra beans to use in Hearty Chicken Stew (page 14) and possibly even Almost Niçoise Salmon Salad (page 16).

SAVE IT FORWARD—HAM STEAK: The remaining half of the ham steak (if using) can be added to tomorrow's Hearty Chicken Stew (page 14).

SAUTÉED SPINACH

1 pound baby spinach (more if you have a larger family or want leftovers)

2 tablespoons olive oil

3 or 4 garlic cloves, minced (or more or less, to taste)

Pinch of cayenne pepper (or skip it if you don't like the heat!)

Table salt, to taste

2 to 3 tablespoons heavy cream (more or less, optional but yummy)

It is shocking how much spinach it takes to make a small amount of sautéed spinach. Thankfully, it's nutritionally dense, so even a small portion is a tremendous source of iron, vitamins A and C, and more. And best of all—it's tasty!

1. Rinse the spinach, even if it is prerinsed, because this will help wilt it. Working in batches, toss the spinach into a dry pan over medium-high heat. Stir and toss to keep it from sticking, and remove it when very wilted. Add the next batch and repeat the process until it is all finished. Set all the wilted spinach aside.

2. In the same pan, heat the oil over medium heat. Add the garlic and cook for a minute until fragrant. Add the spinach back into the pan and toss to coat with the garlicky, oily goodness. Stir in the cayenne and salt. If feeling decadent, add a bit of heavy cream and heat until just warm.

SAVE IT FORWARD— SPINACH: If you have leftover spinach, you can add it to Hearty Chicken Stew (page 14) or to scrambled eggs for breakfast!

HEARTY CHICKEN STEW

8 cups (2 quarts)
Overnight Chicken
Broth (page 268), saved
forward, or other chicken
broth

1½ cups frozen mixed
veggies—carrots, peas,
green beans, and so on

1 cup frozen cut okra
(if you are resolutely
anti-okra, skip it and add
an extra cup of mixed
veggies)

1½ cups Brown Rice Pilaf
(page 9), saved forward

1½ cups Great Northern
Beans (page 11), saved
forward; or use canned

Sautéed Spinach (page
13), saved forward; any
amount you have saved
is fine (or sub a couple of
handfuls of baby spinach)

2 tablespoons tomato
paste (from a tube is so
handy! Less waste!)

1 teaspoon Italian
seasoning

½ teaspoon onion powder

½ teaspoon garlic powder

1 teaspoon kosher salt

½ teaspoon ground black
pepper

This recipe includes okra, and I know many people are anti-okra, but did you know that it's both healthy and weight-loss promoting? Have I convinced you to give it a whirl? It's delicious!

If you are feeding people who want a substantial dinner, you can add buttered and toasted bread, or even a quick grilled cheese, and some sort of fruit on the side.

1 to 2 cups chopped roasted chicken (see page 5), saved forward, or use rotisserie chicken or even canned!

½ to ¾ pound diced ham steak (see page 11), saved forward (optional)

2 tablespoons cornstarch or ¼ cup flour

¼ cup heavy cream (optional, but it really makes it special)

Crusty bread, for serving

1. In a large pot over high heat, bring 7 cups of the chicken broth to a simmer, then add the veggies, okra, rice, beans, spinach, tomato paste, Italian seasoning, onion powder, garlic powder, salt, and pepper. Reduce the heat to medium-low and simmer for 15 minutes, or longer if you like. Add the chicken (and ham, if using).

2. To thicken the soup, make a slurry by whisking the cornstarch or flour into the remaining 1 cup broth (it must be cool) until there are no lumps. Stir slowly into the simmering stew and cook for 5 minutes, stirring occasionally, until thickened a bit. Turn off the heat and stir in the heavy cream (if using).

3. Serve in big bowls with crusty bread on the side; you'll want to sop up all the flavorful broth.

TO DO TONIGHT: *Prep for tomorrow's Almost Niçoise Salmon Salad (page 16): Rinse the lettuce, separate the leaves, and wrap them in a dish towel so they will be crisp but not soggy. If you're feeling super ambitious, you can hard-boil the eggs, too (see page 18).*

ALMOST NIÇOISE SALMON SALAD

2 medium heads of romaine or butter lettuce or another substantial lettuce

Salmon (see page 6), saved forward, lightly warmed

Green beans (see page 6), saved forward, lightly warmed

Great Northern Beans (page 11), saved forward, lightly warmed (or canned beans are just fine!)

Roasted potatoes (see page 3), saved forward, lightly warmed

4 to 6 hard-boiled eggs (one per person), peeled and quartered lengthwise (see page 18)

½ red onion, sliced into thin slivers

2 medium tomatoes, cut into wedges

Olives of your choice (traditionally Niçoise olives!)

Capers (optional, but you'll feel fancy, and their brininess adds a lot of impact)

Everyday Vinaigrette (page 269)

Traditionally, a Niçoise salad will include tuna, but you'll use your leftover salmon instead. Usually, the salad calls for boiled potatoes, but you'll use leftover roasted potatoes from earlier in the week (or just skip them if you don't have any leftovers). Tonight's meal is all about pulling together this week's save-it-forward items, then adding a simple homemade vinaigrette. The only thing you might need to do is boil some eggs if you didn't do so already, or, heck—can't you buy boiled eggs at convenience stores these days?

Personally, I would warm the salmon, green beans, Great Northern beans, and potatoes in the microwave until barely warm. This is sort of a Goldilocks situation: you don't want them too cold, since that would be potentially unappetizing, but you also don't want them too warm, because they're going into a salad. Warm them just until Goldilocks would be happy.

1. A Niçoise salad is traditionally a "composed" salad in which individual ingredients are artistically arranged, as opposed to the usual American jumble of ingredients. For the splashiest arrangement, use a platter for serving, but you can also compose the salad on individual plates. Start with a bed of lettuce as a base layer, then add the components on top—a salmon section, a green bean section, and so on—using all the ingredients. If you want to get really inspired, type "Niçoise Salad images" into Google—wowzers.

2. Drizzle the salad with Everyday Vinaigrette and serve with more dressing on the side.

Hard-Boiled Eggs

If you are like me, you're always on the hunt for the latest scheme for boiling easier-to-peel hard-boiled eggs. Yes, I've tried an Instant Pot, but I think the results are spotty. I've had pretty good luck in an air fryer, of all things (16 minutes at 250°F—no pan to wash!). But not everyone has an air fryer, so my search continued. If you're willing to pay ten bucks for an old-fashioned metal steamer basket, I think you'll be pleased with its usefulness as a hard-boiled-egg cooker. Add an inch of water to a pot and place the steamer basket in the pot. Cover and bring the water to a boil. Add the eggs, cover the pot, and cook for 12 minutes for hard-boiled eggs. Place in ice water to cool and peel under running water for easier removal of the shells.

"EASY LIKE FRIDAY EVENING" PERSONAL PIZZAS

DOUGH (SEE NOTE ON QUANTITIES)

2 cups self-rising flour (see Note on self-rising flour on page 21), plus more for rolling out the dough

2 cups 0% fat Greek yogurt

Cooking spray

SAUCE

One 14.5-ounce can diced fire-roasted (or regular) tomatoes, drained

3 tablespoons tomato paste (a good time to use the tomato paste in a tube!)

1 teaspoon sugar

1 teaspoon minced garlic (jarred is fine)

½ teaspoon dried oregano or Italian seasoning

½ teaspoon balsamic vinegar (optional)

1 or 2 pinches of crushed red pepper flakes

¾ teaspoon table salt

½ teaspoon ground black pepper

TOPPINGS

Grated/shredded cheeses, meats, and veggies of your choice

If you are cooking for a family, I hope homemade pizza will become a Friday night tradition. As a mom of teenagers, I realize how important (and challenging!) it is to create dinnertime traditions to keep your teens connected to the family, particularly when they develop their own busy social lives. There's something innately satisfying about creating a dish together, then eating it around the family table. This pizza sauce and dough are ridiculously simple—even little ones can become handy in the kitchen. Teenagers can invite their friends over for a make-your-own-pizza party!

We like to make personal-size pizzas so family members can add favorite cheeses and toppings. You can fit two personal pizzas on a sheet pan, so if you are feeding six people, it might be easier to just roll out the dough into large rectangles on two sheet pans and cut the pizzas into squares.

This dough recipe is all the rage in Weight Watchers circles, for good reason: the 0% fat Greek yogurt keeps the calories lower and the protein content high. Finally, you can feel virtuous when eating pizza! The health benefits make the dough a tad sticky and harder to work with, though. I have a few tips and tricks to help with that, so be not afraid.

No need to cook the sauce; just whip it up in a blender. It's quick, fresh, healthy, and inexpensive. Or just use jarred sauce—you'll get no judgment from me.

1. Preheat the oven to 400°F.

2. To make the dough, place the flour and Greek yogurt in a large bowl and mix with your hands until the flour is mostly incorporated. (Tip: Spray your hands with cooking spray before you mix!) Turn out the dough and any unincorporated flour onto a generously floured work surface. (If you have a silicone baking mat, it's a great time to use it!) Keep working the dough until all the flour is incorporated. Form the dough into a ball, then divide it evenly into as many pieces as you are making pizzas. Stick the dough in the fridge to briefly chill while you make the sauce.

3. To make the sauce, blend the tomatoes, tomato paste, sugar, garlic, oregano, vinegar (if using), red pepper flakes, salt, and pepper in a blender or a food processor until smooth. (You can freeze any leftovers in ice cube trays for future pizzas, or pop them into your next pot of spaghetti sauce.)

4. Roll out the dough on the well-floured work surface. I use my hands to get the crust mostly rolled out, then I use a well-floured rolling pin to make it thinner. Your goal is a typical thin-crust pizza; if it's too thick, you'll end up with a doughy center.

5. Transfer the rolled-out dough to a sheet pan sprayed with cooking spray (or use the silicone baking mat). Do not make the mistake I did and use foil! You'll be peeling chunks of pizza off the foil to eat (but you'll still do it, because hey, it's still cheesy, gooey pizza, right?).

6. Top the rolled-out dough with sauce and toppings of your choice, then pop it in the oven. When using more than one pan, you may have to switch pans from the top to bottom or bottom to top rack halfway through the baking process to ensure even baking, depending on your oven. Bake for approximately 13 minutes, until the crust is golden brown and the cheese is bubbly.

7. Slice into wedges with a pizza cutter and serve!

NOTE ON QUANTITIES: Depending on people's appetites, a typical serving is ⅓ to ½ cup each of Greek yogurt and self-rising flour. So, a pizza made with 2 cups of flour and 2 cups of yogurt would make between 4 and 6 servings.

NOTE ON SELF-RISING FLOUR: You can make self-rising flour by adding 1½ teaspoons baking powder and ½ teaspoon salt per 1 cup of flour.

NOTE ON GLUTEN-FREE FLOUR: This pizza works well with any gluten-free flour that subs cup for cup with regular flour; just add 1½ teaspoons baking powder and ½ teaspoon salt per 1 cup gluten-free flour.

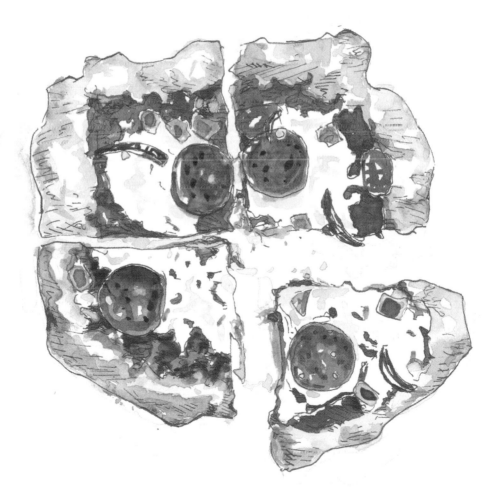

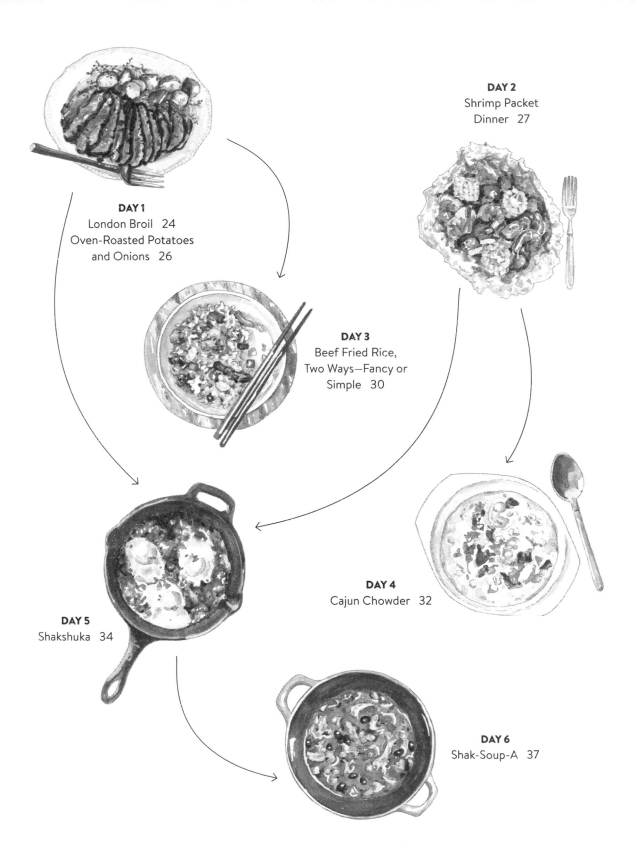

DAY 2
Shrimp Packet
Dinner   27

DAY 1
London Broil   24
Oven-Roasted Potatoes
and Onions   26

DAY 3
Beef Fried Rice,
Two Ways—Fancy or
Simple   30

DAY 4
Cajun Chowder   32

DAY 5
Shakshuka   34

DAY 6
Shak-Soup-A   37

WEEK 2
Surf 'n' Turf 'n' More Week

As I mentioned in the Introduction, I've always tried to broaden my family's palate, and this week is the perfect example of my strategy: balance the familiar and the unfamiliar so I don't have a mutiny on my hands at the dinner table. In the same week I serve Shakshuka, which will arouse my kids' suspicions despite its nifty name, I also serve good ol' American steak and potatoes to pacify my less adventuresome eaters. When it comes to feeding a family, it's all about balance, discernment, and marketing!

LONDON BROIL

Flank steak, 1½ pounds to
3 pounds, depending on
your family size

Table or kosher salt and
cracked or ground black
pepper

*While researching this cookbook, I learned that the term
"London broil" is often misused to describe a cut of meat.
Actually, it's a technique, which we will be using in this
recipe. You might find a piece of beef labeled "London broil"
by the butcher, and if so, grab it and use it for this recipe.
Flank steak will probably be easier to find, though.*

*You'll be cooking the whole flank steak today and saving
forward the leftovers for fried rice, so buy a big enough flank
steak for your family to have two meals (though the fried rice
meal will use less meat—a help to the budget!). Serve with
Oven-Roasted Potatoes and Onions (page 26; see Advance
Prep below).*

1. At least 30 minutes before you'll be cooking, remove the
steak from the fridge and let it come to room temperature.
Salt and pepper the meat liberally on both sides.

2. Meanwhile, preheat the oven to 450°F.

3. Heat a heavy, ovenproof pan (I prefer cast iron) over high
heat until very hot. Add the steak and sear each side for
2 minutes (no oil necessary!).

4. Transfer the pan to the oven and roast for 5 minutes for a
rare steak and 8 to 9 minutes for medium.

ADVANCE PREP: Since they take up to an hour to cook, you could get a head start
on the meal by roasting the potatoes and onions in advance. Roast them until nearly
done, then refrigerate them overnight in their foil. To finish cooking the next day, open
the foil and roast them on a sheet pan while you're cooking the London broil.

5. Check the doneness by slipping in a small knife to look. The meat will be a bit too rare, but it will continue to cook while it rests (step 6). If it is quite a bit too rare for you, pop it back into the oven for a few minutes.

6. Cover and let sit at room temperature for 10 minutes. Cut across the grain into ½-inch slices.

SAVE IT FORWARD—STEAK: You will use the flank steak leftovers for Beef Fried Rice (page 30).

OVEN-ROASTED POTATOES AND ONIONS

2 pounds potatoes (red-skinned or Yukon Gold—whatever you don't have to peel!)

2 medium yellow onions

1 tablespoon butter

1 tablespoon olive oil

Table salt and ground black pepper

Spices and herbs of your choice (garlic powder, paprika, dried parsley, chopped fresh herbs—whatever is on hand)

If you plan to serve the potatoes and onions with the London Broil (page 24), start the recipe about thirty-five minutes before the steak, since it will take about sixty minutes to cook. To eliminate some cleanup, line the sheet pan with foil, mix the ingredients in the pan, and then just toss the foil afterward. If you have a large family, increase the quantities; you'll want leftovers for Shakshuka at the end of the week.

1. Preheat the oven to 400°F (it's okay to share the oven with the London broil's 450°F for a short time). Line a sheet pan with foil.

2. Wash and dry the potatoes and cut them into 1½-inch pieces.

3. Cut each onion into 8 wedges.

4. Melt the butter in a small dish, then add the olive oil.

5. Place the potatoes and onions on the prepared sheet pan, toss with the butter and oil, and season with salt, pepper, and herbs.

6. Roast in the oven for at least 30 minutes undisturbed. You want them nicely browned! Flip the potatoes to keep them from sticking. Depending on the size of the potatoes, they will take at least 15 more minutes to cook, possibly another 30.

SAVE IT FORWARD: Save the leftovers for Shakshuka (page 34).

SHRIMP PACKET DINNER

9 Yukon Gold potatoes (about 3 pounds total; ½ pound per person), or other potatoes, unpeeled and cut into ¾-inch dice

2 small yellow onions, each cut into 6 wedges

18 ounces smoked sausage, cut into 1-inch rounds (a **SAVE-IT-FORWARD** item)

3 ears corn, husked and broken into halves

3 pounds fresh or thawed frozen large shrimp, unpeeled (½ pound per person; a **SAVE-IT-FORWARD** item)

Cajun seasoning

Garlic powder

1 (12-ounce) bottle beer or 1½ cups chicken broth (or water)

Special tool: heavy-duty foil, extra wide is helpful

Did you grow up with foil packet dinners around the campfire? I did, and I have the happy memories to prove it! This recipe brings back all the feels of childhood but with a sophisticated twist. It serves four people with leftovers to make another meal for four of Cajun Chowder (page 32). If your family is bigger, increase the amounts per person according to the notes in the ingredient list.

TO DO TONIGHT:
Prep ingredients for the next couple of meals. (If you're super-allergic to washing dishes, just make these two things in succession with a quick rinse of your pot in between!)

- Cook 5 cups of white or brown rice using your preferred cooking method, for Beef Fried Rice (page 30).
- Make Simple Shrimp Broth (page 29) using the discarded shrimp shells for Cajun Chowder (page 32).

1. Preheat the oven to 375°F.

2. Cut heavy-duty foil into six 20-inch lengths. Make 6 foil packets, 1 per person plus 2 extras for planned leftovers. Be sure to make the packets big enough to encompass all the ingredients, about 5 x 7 inches on the bottom, with enough extra foil at the top to fold over a few times.

3. Divide the ingredients onto each foil sheet in this order: potatoes, onions, sausage, corn, and shrimp. Between the layers, lightly sprinkle Cajun seasoning and a bit of garlic powder. Cup the sides of the foil so that the liquid will not escape and add ¼ cup of the beer to each packet. Accordion fold the excess foil at the top, then fold in the sides to prevent leakage. Set the packets on a sheet pan and bake for 20 minutes.

4. Serve the packets on plates. Be careful when opening the foil—the contents will be hot!

SAVE IT FORWARD—EXTRA PACKETS: Most of the ingredients from the 2 extra packets will be used to make 4 servings of Cajun Chowder (page 32), but reserve all of the smoked sausage and half of the onions for Shakshuka (page 34).

SAVE IT FORWARD—SHRIMP TAILS AND SHELLS: During dinner, make a pile of shells. You will be using them to make Simple Shrimp Broth (page 29) for the chowder.

SIMPLE SHRIMP BROTH

Shrimp shells from
Shrimp Packet Dinner
(page 27)

1 small yellow onion, cut
into wedges (leave the
skin on for richer flavor)

2 carrots, cut into chunks

2 celery stalks, cut into
chunks

2 bay leaves

2 garlic cloves, peeled
and smashed slightly

1 teaspoon black
peppercorns (or
½ teaspoon ground
black pepper)

1 teaspoon table salt
(or to taste)

This is a great use for the shrimp shells scavenged from your dinner guests, as well as from the shrimp in the extra foil packets. (Hey, you rinse and boil the scavenged shells, so calm down, germophobes!)

Put all the ingredients in a large pot, add 6 cups of water or enough to cover the contents, and bring it to boil. Lower the heat to a simmer and cook for at least 30 minutes, then strain the stock and refrigerate (the stock can also be frozen). Discard the solids.

BEEF FRIED RICE, TWO WAYS—FANCY OR SIMPLE

London Broil (page 24), saved forward, sliced into bite-size pieces

1 teaspoon cornstarch

4 tablespoons soy sauce, plus more to taste

3 tablespoons canola oil, or other oil

1 small yellow onion, roughly chopped

2 garlic cloves, minced, or the equivalent from a jar

1 tablespoon grated fresh ginger or ¼ teaspoon ground (optional)

1 to 2 cups chopped uncooked veggies of your choice (see headnote)

5 cups cooked rice

2 eggs

1 tablespoon sesame oil (optional but adds memorable flavor)

Sriracha, to taste (optional)

Depending on your prep time and the people around your table, you can play this two ways: use a package of frozen peas and carrots for the quick-and-dirty, kid-friendly version. If you want a more sophisticated adult version, try Brussels sprouts! Or, go rogue with the veggies of your choice: broccoli, mushrooms, whatever strikes your fancy! Depending on the density of your veggie, please note that your cooking time will vary a bit.

1. In a large bowl, toss the leftover beef with the cornstarch, then with 2 tablespoons of the soy sauce. Let it marinate while you prepare the rest of the ingredients.

2. Heat a deep, wide skillet over medium heat. Heat ½ tablespoon of the oil, then add the onion and cook until it starts to get translucent, about 2 minutes. Add the garlic and ginger and cook for another minute. Add the steak and cook for 2 to 3 minutes. Transfer the beef and onion to the bowl in which you marinated the meat.

3. Heat another ½ tablespoon of the oil and add the veggies of your choice. Sauté until barely cooked; they should still be a bit firm. Remove to the bowl with the meat.

4. Add 1 tablespoon of oil to the pan and heat it over medium-high heat until it begins smoking. Add the rice, with a tablespoon or so of water as needed to help break it apart. Stir occasionally to keep the rice from sticking, but let it sear and brown in the pan a bit.

5. When the rice is heated through, turn the heat to medium-low and return the meat and veggies to the pan. Make a well in the rice and crack in the eggs. Stir to scramble the eggs, then integrate them into the rice mixture. Add the remaining 2 tablespoons soy sauce and the sesame oil, if using, and stir to combine.

6. Serve with additional soy sauce and with sriracha, if desired, for extra flavor and heat.

CAJUN CHOWDER

2 packets from Shrimp
Packet Dinner (page 27),
saved forward

Simple Shrimp Broth
(page 29)

4 bacon slices, roughly
chopped

Table salt and ground
black pepper

¼ cup heavy cream (or
half-and-half or even
whole milk)

Grated cheddar (or
other) cheese, for garnish
(optional)

Sliced green onions, for
garnish (optional)

*As written, this recipe serves four people, so increase
quantities accordingly if you saved extra shrimp packets
forward for extra eaters. Figure one extra packet for every
two servings.*

1. Extract the ingredients from the foil packcts. Chop the
shrimp into small-ish pieces, scrape the corn off the cob,
and chop ½ cup of the leftover onion. Reserve 1½ cups of
potatoes to be added to the soup in chunks and place the
rest of the potatoes into a blender or into a container for
immersion blending. (See the note on page 33 about saving
forward the sausage and the rest of the onion.)

2. Pour the broth from the packets over the potatoes in the blender. Add 1 cup of the shrimp broth to the potatoes and blend until smooth. The potatoes will thicken the broth.

3. In a large saucepan over medium heat, sauté the bacon until lightly browned. (If you want to get a little fancy, save a bit of bacon to sprinkle on top of the soup when serving.) Add the ½ cup chopped onion and sauté for a few minutes more, until the onion is soft and the bacon is fully cooked.

4. Over medium heat, add to the pan 5 cups of the shrimp broth, the contents of the blender, the reserved 1½ cups potato chunks, the corn kernels, and the chopped shrimp. Heat through, taste, and add salt and pepper as needed. Turn off the heat, add the cream, and stir. Divide among bowls, topping if desired with reserved bacon and with cheese and green onions.

SAVE IT FORWARD—SAUSAGE AND ONION: Save the leftover sausage and the remainder of the onion for Shakshuka (page 34).

SHAKSHUKA

½ tablespoon olive oil

½ cup chopped yellow onion (see page 32), saved forward

1 bell pepper (I like red or orange), cut into medium dice

3 or 4 kale leaves, stemmed and sliced into thin ribbons (optional, but a way to sneak in some healthy greens)

6 ounces smoked sausage, cut into ½-inch rounds (see page 27), saved forward; omit for a meatless meal

½ to 1 jalapeño, finely diced

2 teaspoons minced garlic

1 to 2 teaspoons table salt

1 teaspoon smoked (or regular) paprika

One 28-ounce can diced tomatoes (I like fire-roasted)

2 tablespoons tomato paste (the kind in a tube is handy for this amount!)

Oven-Roasted Potatoes and Onions (page 26), saved forward

Eggs, as many as desired by your dining companions

Crumbled feta cheese (optional, for serving)

Don't be intimidated by the name; Shakshuka is the simplest and most delicious meal. It's really just a flavorful, thick tomato sauce with eggs cooked on top. It's a Middle Eastern dish, though the Italians have adopted it and named it Eggs in Purgatory, probably because it would be the perfect meatless Lenten meal for Catholics.

Many recipes call for this dish to be cooked on the stove with a lid, basically poaching the eggs in the sauce. I found that it's a little more streamlined to cook it uncovered in the oven: the eggs seem to benefit by not having the condensation of the covered pan. If you don't have an ovenproof pan, however, the stovetop method works just fine!

Shakshuka is often served with bread to sop up the tomato juices, but here I call for leftover potatoes and onions to serve as the base.

1. Preheat the oven to 375°F.

2. In a deep, ovenproof skillet over medium heat, heat the oil. Add the onion, pepper, kale, sausage, and jalapeño and sauté until the veggies start to soften. Add the garlic, salt, sugar, and paprika and sauté for 1 to 2 minutes, until the garlic is fragrant. Add the tomatoes and tomato paste and cook, stirring often, for 10 minutes or so, to combine the flavors.

3. Make a well in the tomato sauce for each egg and crack the eggs into the wells. Carefully place the pan in the oven and cook for 10 minutes or a bit more, depending on how runny you like your yolks. The whites should no longer be translucent.

4. At the same time that you place the eggs in the oven, reheat the leftover potatoes and onions in a small pan in the oven (you'll also need room for the pan with the eggs). They should be ready when the eggs finish, but they may need a bit more time.

5. Serve the Shakshuka over the potatoes and onions. Sprinkle with a bit of crumbled feta, if you like (I do!).

SAVE IT FORWARD—TOMATO SAUCE: Save the extra Shakshuka sauce, minus the sausage (about 1½ cups) for Shak-Soup-A (page 37), the quickest soup *ever*!

SHAK-SOUP-A

Tomato sauce from Shakshuka (page 34), saved forward

4 cups Overnight Chicken Broth (page 268) or other chicken broth (if you have less tomato sauce left, use less broth; the soup should be tomatoey)

One 12.5-ounce can cooked chicken (don't be afraid—no one will know!)

Half a 15-ounce can of black beans, drained (about 1 cup)

1 cup frozen or drained canned corn

Seriously, this is the easiest tomato soup ever! Just grab your leftover Shakshuka sauce and some pantry ingredients and you're fifteen minutes away from a home-cooked soup.

Combine all the ingredients in a saucepan and heat over medium heat until warmed, and congratulate yourself for buying this book!

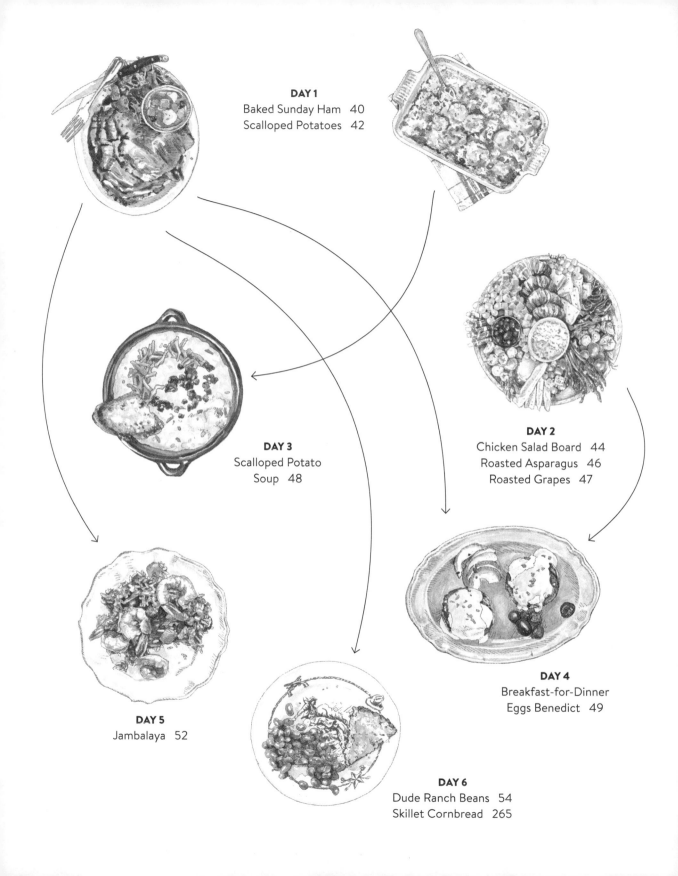

DAY 1
Baked Sunday Ham   40
Scalloped Potatoes   42

DAY 2
Chicken Salad Board   44
Roasted Asparagus   46
Roasted Grapes   47

DAY 3
Scalloped Potato
Soup   48

DAY 4
Breakfast-for-Dinner
Eggs Benedict   49

DAY 5
Jambalaya   52

DAY 6
Dude Ranch Beans   54
Skillet Cornbread   265

Big Ol' Honkin' Ham Week!

We've all heard of Shark Week, but have you heard of Ham Week? No? Well, welcome to the week where several meals launch from one honker of a ham, with the help of one tiny chicken. If it's the end of the month and you're strapped for cash, Ham Week will save your bacon and pull your fat out of the fire. (Oh, wow . . . super bad mom joke!)

ADVANCE PREP: Tackle these simple but time-consuming Save-It-Forward basics on the weekend and have them ready for easy weeknight eating!

Everyday Slow-Cooker Chicken

Stick a whole chicken in the slow cooker so you can have it for a couple of meals this week (page 266). It doesn't need to be pretty, so no need to roast it. Of course, a store-bought rotisserie chicken is a brilliant option as well. The breasts will be used for Chicken Salad Board (page 44); the remainder will be used for Jambalaya (page 52).

Overnight Chicken Broth

Since you'll have chicken bones already, it's a snap to go ahead and make broth (page 268) for this week's Scalloped Potato Soup (page 48), which will make it more economical, flavorful, and healthful. Or ditch all those virtuous attributes and put a carton of chicken broth on your grocery list—no judgment here!

BAKED SUNDAY HAM

One 5- to 7-pound fully cooked bone-in ham (a **SAVE-IT-FORWARD** item; if you use a boneless ham, you'll need a ham hock later for the Dude Ranch Beans on page 54)

Doesn't this meal take you back to a simpler time when mothers wore aprons and fathers smoked pipes? I'm not advocating that, per se, but a Sunday dinner just like at Grandma's house brings a comforting nostalgia to the family table. You'll need to purchase a rather large ham (referred to as "honkin'" in the weekly meal plan) because you'll use all of it during Ham Week but just a modest piece or two tonight.

Also, I need to mention at the outset that Okies, unless they are imposters, do not eat sweet meats. So, I am not not not including a glaze in this recipe. Nope. If you are from a region that eats a sweet ham glaze, you will just have to call your grandma. If she's not alive, I guess my only advice would be to warm some orange marmalade in the microwave and baste your perfectly good ham with it? I don't know. I'm washing my hands of the matter.

Along with Scalloped Potatoes (page 42) and Frozen Fruit Cups (page 275), this meal pairs well with a simple green salad or sautéed zucchini.

Yes, there is just one ingredient in this recipe.

1. Preheat the oven to 350°F.

2. Cut individual slices from the ham appropriate for your family's meal tonight. Cover and refrigerate the rest of the ham for later in the week.

3. The only bad thing that can happen when you reheat a ham is that it can turn out too dry. You need to go on the offensive with a strategy: use a baking pan with a rack set in it and add an inch of water to the pan.

4. Place the ham slices on a large piece of foil and fold the edges up, leaving the top open. Place the ham on the rack, then cover the entire pan with foil. Cook for at least 30 minutes, until warmed through (mine took 45 minutes; it depends on the size of your slices).

SAVE IT FORWARD: Reserve the remaining ham for use in Breakfast-for-Dinner Eggs Benedict (page 49) and Jambalaya (page 52).

SCALLOPED POTATOES

Cooking spray

3 tablespoons butter

1 large yellow onion, cut into ½-inch dice

2 tablespoons white vinegar (or any light-colored vinegar)

3 cups milk

¼ cup flour (gluten-free works fine)

1 teaspoon chicken base, or ½ teaspoon additional table salt

⅛ teaspoon cayenne pepper

½ teaspoon garlic powder

½ teaspoon table salt

½ teaspoon seasoned salt, or ¼ teaspoon additional table salt

½ teaspoon ground black pepper

3 pounds Yukon Gold or other potatoes, sliced ⅛ inch thick (see Note on page 43)

2½ cups freshly shredded good melty cheese (not aged), such as cheddar

1. Preheat the oven to 350°F. Spray a 9 x 13-inch pan with cooking spray.

2. In a large, deep skillet or Dutch oven, melt the butter. Add the onion and cook over medium heat for 3 minutes, until translucent. Add the vinegar and bring it to a boil, stirring and scraping up those browned bits of goodness. Continue stirring until the vinegar has evaporated.

3. Place the milk in a medium bowl and whisk in the flour and chicken base until smooth. Add the milk mixture to the onion mixture, whisking constantly. Continue stirring and cooking until thickened and starting to get bubbly, about 3 minutes. You don't want it to come to a full boil.

4. Remove from the heat and stir in the cayenne, garlic powder, salt, seasoned salt, and pepper. Add the potatoes and toss until they are coated in sauce.

5. Spread half of the potato mixture evenly in the pan, using your hands to be sure the potato slices are separated, then top with half the cheese. Top with the rest of the potatoes and the rest of the cheese.

6. Bake uncovered for 60 to 75 minutes, until the potatoes are tender and the top is golden brown. The thinner the potato slices are, the faster they're likely to bake. Test the potatoes with a fork; if they are still a tad crunchy but getting too browned on top, cover with foil and continue baking. (The outside edges will finish baking first, and you can serve the potatoes from there. Since you'll be using the leftovers for soup later in the week, the middle can stay a tad undercooked.)

NOTE: I like Yukon Gold potatoes because you don't have to peel them if you wash them well. If you have a mandoline or a food processor with a slicer, using either tool is definitely the easiest way to slice the potatoes to thin perfection. If you have mad knife skills, you can slice the potatoes by hand, but be careful! I bought a cut-resistant glove on Amazon and can now use the mandoline with wild abandon without slicing my fingers.

SAVE IT FORWARD: Cover the leftovers in foil and refrigerate until it's time to make Scalloped Potato Soup (page 48).

CHICKEN SALAD BOARD

2 cooked chicken breasts
(see page 39), roughly
chopped

¾ cup mayonnaise, plus
more as desired

¼ cup finely chopped
pickles

Juice of ½ to 1 lemon

Table salt and ground
black pepper

Crisp romaine leaves

Bread of your choice
(we like Hawaiian rolls)

Roasted Asparagus
(page 46)

Roasted Grapes (page 47)

Other accompaniments
for the board: a variety of
olives, pickles, cheeses,
veggies, and crackers

In my younger, sillier, more idealistic years of motherhood, I used to try to serve my family the kind of chicken salad that caught my fancy in college—grapes, poppy seeds, the works. Let's just say that my boys always ate a peanut butter sandwich right after dinner. Then I stumbled upon a chicken salad that we could all agree on. More like a spread than a salad, it lends itself to a creative presentation, on one of those fun boards served with a crock of the chicken salad, Hawaiian rolls, an array of cheeses, pickles, along with some beautifully roasted asparagus spears and a dish of roasted grapes. Your family dinner will feel like a party!

1. Like the Breakfast-for-Dinner Eggs Benedict later in the week, this is more of a method than a recipe. Here's my trick: use a mixer to combine the chicken and mayo until it has a smooth, spreadable consistency. Mix in the pickles along with the lemon juice and salt and pepper to taste. Getting the flavor just right is more an art than a science; keep tasting as you go. Place the chicken salad in a bowl on a large board or platter.

2. Serve with crisp romaine, bread, and extra mayo for people to make their own sandwiches. Add the Roasted Asparagus, Roasted Grapes, and other accompaniments to the board to round out the party at your table.

Shameless plug: If you need a fabulous board, I have one for you!
I partnered with Sandy from Reluctant Entertainer to make the
best darn board on the market. Go to houseofhyacinth.com for the
board and reluctantentertainer.com for amazing presentation ideas.
Thank you for allowing me this commercial break!

ROASTED ASPARAGUS

Fresh asparagus, preferably medium-size spears

1 to 2 tablespoons olive oil, depending on the amount of asparagus

Table salt and ground black pepper

Lemon juice (optional)

These asparagus are terrific to help round out the Chicken Salad Board (page 44). Make however much you like, but you'll be making hollandaise sauce tomorrow, so any extra roasted asparagus will have a delicious accompaniment.

1. Preheat the oven to 400°F.

2. Line a sheet pan with foil. Place the asparagus on the pan. Drizzle with olive oil, toss, add salt and pepper to taste, and spread the asparagus into a single layer. Roast for at least 10 minutes, until lightly browned; thicker stalks will take longer.

3. If you have a lemon in your fridge, a squirt at the end before serving is nice! These can be served warm or at room temperature.

SAVE IT FORWARD—ASPARAGUS: Save any extra Roasted Asparagus for an accompaniment to Breakfast-for-Dinner Eggs Benedict (page 49).

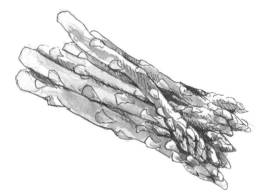

ROASTED GRAPES

1 tablespoon olive oil

2 cups seedless red grapes

Seriously . . . just try these. Once you do, you'll lament all the lost years without them. You'll love them with cheese and crackers as part of your Chicken Salad Board (page 44), but try them the next morning on top of peanut butter toast or mixed into yogurt.

1. Preheat the oven to 400°F.

2. Line a sheet pan with foil. Place the grapes on the pan and toss with the oil. Roast for 20 minutes (but check at 15 minutes if your grapes are small). There's no official done with these: the skin will likely burst on most of them, but just taste to see if they are to your liking.

SCALLOPED POTATO SOUP

3 or 4 bacon slices, chopped

1 large carrot, peeled and roughly chopped

2 celery stalks, roughly chopped

4 cups Scalloped Potatoes (page 42), saved forward

4 cups Overnight Chicken Broth (page 268), or other chicken broth

½ cup heavy cream or half-and-half (optional; see Note)

Table salt and ground black pepper

Shredded cheddar cheese, for serving

Leftover scalloped potatoes reimagined as potato soup—cool, eh? Butter and toast your favorite bread to serve alongside, and if you have any Frozen Fruit Cups (page 275) on hand, it's a full meal!

1. In a large skillet over medium heat, fry the bacon until lightly browned, about 5 minutes. Set aside. Drain some of the bacon grease if you like (I don't!), add the carrots and celery, and sauté until tender, another 5 to 7 minutes. Add the scalloped potatoes and chicken broth and use a spatula to chop up the potato slices until they are a size that suits you.

2. Cover the pan, bring to a simmer, and cook for 15 to 20 minutes, stirring occasionally, until the flavors meld together. Stir in the cream and add salt and pepper to taste.

3. Serve in big bowls with the reserved bacon bits and a sprinkle of shredded cheese.

NOTE ON CREAM:
This soup is very good without the cream. It will be brothier and a bit less rich, and the color will be not quite as pretty.

BREAKFAST-FOR-DINNER EGGS BENEDICT

Eggs

Two 1.25-ounce packages McCormick Hollandaise Sauce Mix, or brand of your choice (see Note on page 51)

8 tablespoons (1 stick) butter, plus more for buttering the bread

Juice of 1 lemon

English muffins

Baked Sunday Ham (page 40), saved forward

Paprika, for garnish

Roasted Asparagus (page 46), saved forward, for serving

Special tool: silicone egg-poaching cups (optional)

This recipe is pretty elementary, but I rarely hear of anyone making Eggs Benedict at home, and you should be. Honestly, this is our family's go-to special meal on Sundays or breakfast-for-dinner treat. I include it here because it's a great tradition to start with your family and friends; your lives will be enriched and your pants enlarged. (Kidding! I kid! Your pants will be just fine.)

I have "dummified" this recipe—it's truly foolproof! True confession: I have never been able to make hollandaise from scratch that was as good as hollandaise from a package. I was vindicated when a highly trained chef pal of mine told me that she always makes it from a packaged mix but also employs a secret chef trick: a squeeze of fresh lemon juice.

1. Turn on the oven broiler (set it to low if you can).

2. Set a large pan of water over high heat for the poached eggs.

3. To make the hollandaise sauce, follow the package directions, using the 8 tablespoons of butter, but at the end, add a squeeze of lemon juice. I generally add the juice from half a lemon per package of hollandaise, but taste as you add the lemon juice gradually.

4. To make the English muffins, fork them open and butter the open faces. Stick them under the broiler, but keep an eye on them because they burn quickly. Don't be afraid to get them really browned, though. (I usually delegate this task to one of my kids because Eggs Benedict has many moving parts for the cook.)

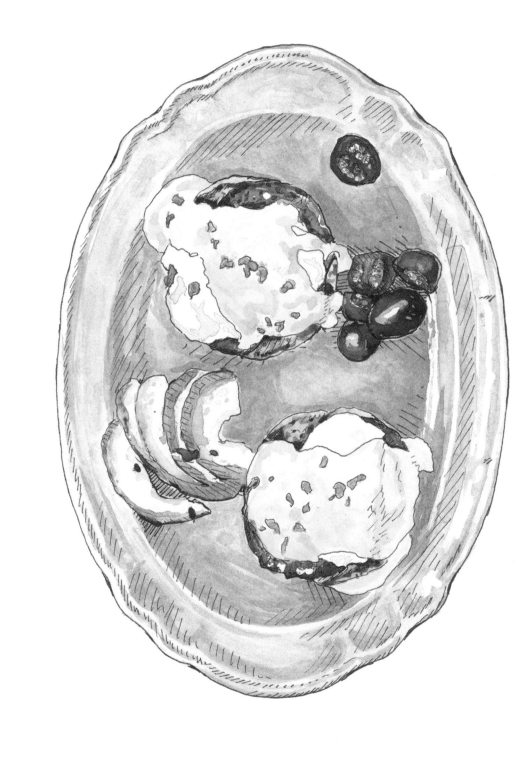

5. Reheat the ham however you like: in a skillet on low heat with a little bit of water, or on a cast-iron griddle, or sprinkled with a little bit of water and wrapped in foil and heated in the oven for a bit. Heck, you can even microwave it.

6. If you have silicone egg cups, simply crack an egg into each cup and slip the cup into gently boiling water. (Violently boiling water will slosh up into your eggs, and then you'll have to drain it off.) Otherwise, stir the simmering water to make a vortex, crack an egg into it, turn off the heat, cover the pan, and leave undisturbed for 5 minutes. I have never been successful at this vortex method, so I use the silicone cups. Or, just make slightly runny fried eggs!

7. For each English muffin half, top with a slice of ham and a poached egg, then slather it generously with hollandaise. A sprinkle of paprika makes it pretty!

DISCLAIMER: For our family, the serving and eating process is a bit raucous because . . . hmm . . . maybe we are uncivilized barbarians? My pan holds only four egg cups at a time, and my boys always want two rounds, so I'm standing at the stove, poaching more eggs while they are wolfing down the first round and sliding their plates to me for their second. After they finish their second serving, they invariably look up and say, "Wait . . . Mom, have you eaten yet?" Honestly, their enjoyment is such a joy that I don't care that I'm the last eater (as long as they will stay at the table and talk to me!).

NOTE ON THE HOLLANDAISE MIX: With any luck you will have some leftover hollandaise sauce for that leftover asparagus. Each package makes 1 cup of sauce, and the manufacturer claims 2 tablespoons is a serving . . . *pshaw*. Just buy 2 packages and send me a thank-you card later.

JAMBALAYA

2 tablespoons olive oil

¾ pound ham (see page 40), saved forward, cut into bite-size chunks (about 2 cups)

2 cups 1-inch-diced cooked chicken (see page 39), saved forward

1 green or red bell pepper, cut into ½-inch dice

1 yellow onion, cut into ½-inch dice

2 celery stalks, thinly sliced

3 garlic cloves, minced (jarred is fine)

1 tablespoon Cajun seasoning

2 teaspoons Worcestershire sauce

One 15-ounce can crushed tomatoes

½ to 1 teaspoon hot pepper sauce, depending on your taste

½ teaspoon table salt, plus more to taste

½ teaspoon ground black pepper, plus more to taste

1¼ cups uncooked white rice (or brown rice; see Note)

3 cups Overnight Chicken Broth (page 268), saved forward, or other chicken broth

I lived in New Orleans for a time during high school and developed a love of Cajun cuisine. I lived there long enough to say with certainty that my version is not authentically Cajun because, for one thing, it doesn't include filé powder, which most of you probably won't have on hand. Filé is a thickening agent, so in lieu of that, I used okra, which is very authentic and will help thicken the dish a bit. If you are violently anti-okra, I will turn my head and pretend like I don't see you eschewing the okra. Even though not technically authentic, this dish has incredible flavor, and best of all, it uses save-it-forward components, which significantly lessen the work!

One 12-ounce bag defrosted frozen okra

1 cup medium fresh or defrosted frozen raw shrimp, peeled (optional; see Note)

TO DO TONIGHT:
For tomorrow's Dude Ranch Beans (page 54), place 1 pound of pinto beans in the slow cooker, cover with water by about 3 inches, and let sit overnight (don't turn the slow cooker on).

1. Heat 1 tablespoon of the olive oil in a Dutch oven or other large pot over medium heat. Add the ham and chicken and lightly brown, 3 to 4 minutes. Remove from the pan and set aside. Heat the remaining 1 tablespoon of oil and add the bell pepper, onion, celery, and garlic. Sprinkle with the Cajun seasoning and cook, stirring often, until the vegetables are slightly softened, 3 to 5 minutes. Return the ham and chicken to the pan.

2. Add the Worcestershire sauce, tomatoes, and hot sauce, and cook for 5 minutes, stirring occasionally. Sprinkle with the salt and pepper.

3. Add the rice and chicken broth and stir. Bring to a boil, reduce the heat to medium-low, cover, and simmer for about 20 minutes, or until the liquid is absorbed. Stir occasionally to keep the rice from sticking. Add the okra and shrimp and cook for 5 minutes, until the okra is tender and the shrimp has just turned pink.

4. Taste to make sure the rice is tender. If it is still a bit crunchy, add ½ cup more broth or water and cook for 3 to 4 more minutes. Adjust the seasonings and serve.

NOTE: To substitute brown rice, cook it separately and add with the okra and the shrimp.

NOTE: Shrimp is a fun addition if you happen to have a bag of frozen shrimp handy. While I'm chopping the veggies, I place the shrimp in a strainer in the sink and run warm water over them until they thaw.

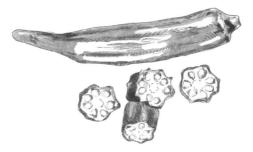

DUDE RANCH BEANS

1 pound dried pinto beans

Ham bone from the week's ham (see page 40), saved forward, or a ham hock, if your ham was boneless

One 8-ounce can tomato sauce or 3 tablespoons tomato paste

1 medium yellow onion, cut into ½-inch dice

1 large or 2 small dried chiles (see Note)

2 medium garlic cloves, minced

2 tablespoons chili powder

1 teaspoon table salt, plus more to taste

1 teaspoon ground black pepper, plus more to taste

Before I was born, my parents made frequents treks to a Colorado dude ranch for family vacations. I came along after these trips, but I did end up with their famous bean recipe instead of an ugly T-shirt, which worked out perfectly for me. If you think beans are not your thing, give this recipe a try— it has a certain ranch-y flair that I think you'll like. Beans and cornbread are inseparable friends, and you can find my favorite cornbread recipe on page 265. This is a wonderfully frugal meal if you have more month than money!

Soak the beans overnight as directed on page 53. Drain the water in the morning and add fresh water to cover the beans by 2 inches. Add the ham bone, tomato sauce, onion, chile, garlic, chili powder, salt, and pepper and cook on low all day, 6 to 8 hours, until the beans are tender. Toward the end, you can remove the meat from the ham bone and add it to the beans, but the beans will be delightfully flavorful without it, too. Taste the beans to see if they need more salt and pepper.

NOTE ON CHILES: The chiles are often found with packaged Mexican spices. I used a guajillo chile, which is smoky but not hot.

DAY 1
Chipotle Chicken   58

DAY 2
Cheater's Posole   60
Jalapeño Poppers   62

DAY 3
Open-Faced Bacon, Tomato,
and Cheese Sandwiches   64
Cucumber Salad   66

DAY 4
Skillet Smoked Sausage,
Cabbage, and Potatoes   67

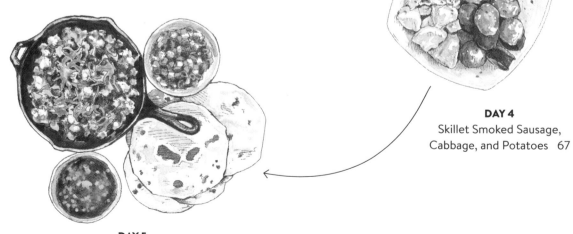

DAY 5
Breakfast-for-Dinner Burritos   68

WEEK 4
No Time to Spare Week!

When you know you're facing a crazy week, this week's menu will keep you out of the drive-through lanes. The slow cooker (or Instant Pot) will save your life for a couple of meals, and the rest of the week consists of simple skillet dishes and sandwiches. No regrets at the end of the week, for your budget or your waistline!

OVERACHIEVER IDEA

Make a fancy sauce or dip! If you're feeling ambitious, make Hamlin's White Sauce (page 272), Chipotle Cream Sauce (page 273), or Peruvian Green Sauce (page 274) over the weekend to kick your Chipotle Chicken (page 58) to a new level. They'd also be perfect for the Breakfast-for-Dinner Burritos (page 68)—or for snacking with tortilla chips all week!

CHIPOTLE CHICKEN

¼ to ½ cup canned chipotle chiles in adobo sauce, depending on your heat preference (from one 7-ounce can; measure both chiles and sauce)

One 7-ounce can salsa verde

2 tablespoons lime juice

1 tablespoon liquid smoke (you can skip it, but it does make this dish unique)

1 medium yellow onion, cut into ½-inch dice

2 teaspoons garlic powder

2 teaspoons sugar

1 teaspoon table salt

1 teaspoon dried oregano

2 pounds boneless skinless chicken breasts

Tortilla chips or corn or flour tortillas, for serving

Optional but fun toppings and garnishes: shredded cheese, salsa, sour cream, chopped cilantro, lime wedges

Optional saved-forward sauces, for serving: Hamlin's White Sauce (page 272), Chipotle Cream Sauce (page 273), or Peruvian Green Sauce (page 274)

This is my twist on the classic shredded chicken recipe with various uses: burritos, tacos, nachos—just make your own Mexican fiesta bar! Though it seems like a lot of chicken, you'll be saving forward some of it for tomorrow night's posole, and you may have enough for a lunch salad or taco. You can throw this in the slow cooker in the morning, but it's also a nifty Instant Pot recipe.

TO DO TONIGHT:
Crumble and brown the sausage for tomorrow's Cheater's Posole (page 60).

1. In a slow cooker or Instant Pot, combine the chipotle chiles, salsa verde, lime juice, liquid smoke (if using), onion, garlic powder, sugar, salt, and oregano. Place the chicken in the cooker and coat with the sauce. If using a slow cooker, cook for 6 to 8 hours on low or 4 to 6 hours on high. If using an Instant Pot, cook for 15 minutes on high pressure, then do a quick release. You should be able to easily pierce and shred the chicken with a fork.

2. Shred the chicken with two forks or whatever ingenious method you generally employ. Serve with tortilla chips or in corn or flour tortillas, along with your favorite toppings. If you made one of the suggested sauces, now is the time to drizzle it liberally over all!

SAVE IT FORWARD—CHICKEN: Reserve 2 cups of shredded chicken for tomorrow's Cheater's Posole (page 60).

CHEATER'S POSOLE

6 cups (1½ quarts) Overnight Chicken Broth (page 268) or other chicken broth, plus more as needed

1 pound hot or mild breakfast sausage, cooked, crumbled, and drained (reserve some as a **SAVE-IT-FORWARD** item for Jalapeño Poppers, page 62, if desired)

2 cups shredded Chipotle Chicken (page 58), saved forward

1 bay leaf

2 dry guajillo chiles (or other mild dried chiles, or 2 teaspoons chipotle chile powder)

½ teaspoon ground cumin

1 teaspoon dried oregano

Two 15½-ounce cans hominy (I used 1 can of white and 1 can of yellow), drained and rinsed

One 11-ounce can shoepeg corn, drained

Optional tasty toppings: sour cream, sliced avocado, sliced radishes, shredded cabbage, crushed tortilla chips, cilantro

I was first introduced to posole at a church potluck when I was a young bride. The elderly lady who brought it gave me very vague instructions—"A little of this, a little of that"—so I've never been able to re-create her recipe. Since real posole takes several hours, and I'm always looking for a shortcut, I developed this recipe that scratches my posole itch in a much shorter time. Serve with Jalapeño Poppers (page 62).

1. For the slow cooker: Place the broth, sausage, chicken, bay leaf, chiles, cumin, oregano, hominy, and corn in the slow cooker and cook for 4 to 6 hours on low, or even all day. For the Instant Pot: Place all the ingredients (except the toppings) in the pot and cook on high pressure for 10 minutes, then do a quick release.

2. Taste the soup for seasonings and add a bit more broth if you like it brothier. Discard the bay leaf.

3. To make the soup really special, serve with the optional toppings.

JALAPEÑO POPPERS (OR MINI PEPPER POPPERS)

6 jalapeños or mini bell peppers

4 ounces cream cheese, softened slightly

¾ cup grated cheese of your choice, such as cheddar

½ cup cooked and crumbled breakfast sausage (see page 60), saved forward (optional)

4 or 6 bacon slices (see Note on page 63)

Pretty much everyone loves these, right? Typically an appetizer item, they also make a perfect side dish for soup—and my men always want something a little more substantial than just a bowl of soup. You probably have a popper recipe already, but I'm including my simple one just in case, and I've also added some optional tweaks: For a less spicy version, use mini bell peppers! Add sausage! One time I chopped up a fresh peach and added it to the cream cheese mixture (and skipped the grated cheese), and it was really good!

1. Preheat the oven to 400°F and cover a sheet pan with foil. Add a wire rack on top if you have one.

2. Slice the jalapeños in half lengthwise and remove the seeds. (I use plastic food storage or grocery bags to cover my hands during the popper preparation process. You only have to rub your eyes with jalapeño hands once before you take precautionary measures.)

3. In a medium bowl, mix the cream cheese and cheese and sausage, if using.

4. Fill the jalapeño halves with the cream cheese mixture, then wrap each with half a bacon slice. I never bother to secure with a toothpick; just tuck the ends under the popper. Make sure to tuck well so the bacon doesn't curl up. Set the poppers on the wire rack (or directly on the foil) as you go.

5. Bake for 20 to 25 minutes, or until the bacon is cooked to your liking.

NOTE ON BACON: I generally use ½ slice of bacon per popper, though you could get by with ⅓ slice. Bacon will be used the next day on Open-Faced Bacon, Tomato, and Cheese Sandwiches (page 64), and you'll need 1½ slices per sandwich. If you want to use just one bacon package for the week, you may want to skimp a little on tonight's poppers.

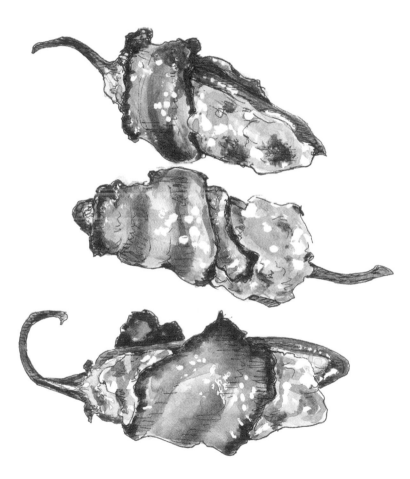

OPEN-FACED BACON, TOMATO, AND CHEESE SANDWICHES

1½ bacon slices per sandwich

Bread, lightly toasted

1 cheese slice per sandwich (your choice! American singles, cheddar, Velveeta—don't be a hater!)

Sliced tomatoes

Sliced avocado (optional)

Did you know you can cook bacon in the oven? If this is a moment of epiphany for you, I predict that your life will never be the same (or at least the part of your life that involves bacon). This is one of my favorite comfort foods from childhood, and I love it even more today because it's a quick meal that seems to please everyone. Paired with Cucumber Salad (page 66), your meal will be mostly vegetables, with just enough bacon to soothe the carnivorous types.

1. Preheat the oven to 400°F with a rack toward the top.

2. To cook the bacon in the oven, line a sheet pan with foil (extra wide works perfectly, and you won't even have to wash the pan!). Lay the bacon on the pan and cook for 18 to 20 minutes, until slightly undercooked and still soft (it will cook for a bit longer under the broiler). Drain the bacon on paper towels to remove extra grease.

3. Drain the grease from the pan. (Are you the kind of person who keeps a jar of bacon grease in the fridge? You can use it to add flavor to all sorts of things—give it a shot!)

4. Turn the oven setting to broil (low if you have that option).

5. Remove the foil from the sheet pan and use the pan to assemble the sandwiches: bread on the bottom, then cheese, then tomato, then bacon.

6. Place the sandwiches under the broiler and broil until the bacon is fully cooked, watching them closely so they don't burn. The bacon will crisp up a bit and add some delicious bacon drippings to your sandwich. If the bread gets too dark on the edges, just cut that away before serving.

7. Add sliced avocados for serving for a bit more color and texture, if desired.

CUCUMBER SALAD

2 cucumbers, peeled and cut into ½-inch slices

2 Roma tomatoes, cut into 1-inch chunks, or 10 cherry tomatoes, halved

¼ medium red onion, thinly sliced

¼ cup Hamlin's White Sauce (page 272), saved forward, or bottled ranch or blue cheese dressing

2 tablespoons buttermilk or milk, plus more as needed

Fresh thyme leaves or minced fresh basil leaves (optional)

Table salt and ground black pepper

I'm a fan of lettuce-less salads—what about you? Though this has a classic summer vibe, it works well as a winter salad because the ingredients are so readily available year-round. If you can't find in-season tomatoes, use cherry tomatoes for a burst of flavor.

1. Place the cucumbers, tomatoes, and onion in a serving bowl.

2. Thin the Hamlin's sauce with the buttermilk, whisking or shaking in a jar to combine. (No need to thin bottled dressing.)

3. Pour the sauce over the veggies until you achieve your perfect ratio of dressing to veggies, toss, and taste, adding fresh herbs, salt, and pepper to your liking.

SKILLET SMOKED SAUSAGE, CABBAGE, AND POTATOES

2 cups Overnight Chicken Broth (page 268), or other chicken broth, or chicken base and water to make 2 cups

1½ pounds good-quality smoked sausage, bratwurst, kielbasa, or similar sausage (a **SAVE-IT-FORWARD** item)

2 pounds potatoes (Yukon Gold or red new potatoes, for a no-peel option; a **SAVE-IT-FORWARD** item)

½ head green cabbage, cored

Table salt and ground black pepper

Butter, for serving

SAVE IT FORWARD— POTATOES AND SAUSAGE: Save the leftover potatoes and sausage for Breakfast-for-Dinner Burritos (page 68).

This is embarrassingly simple, but my family loves it. You'll cook extra sausage and potatoes, which will morph into breakfast for dinner tomorrow night!

1. In a large, deep skillet over medium-high heat, bring the chicken broth or chicken base and water to a simmer.

2. Cut the sausage into serving-size portions. Cut the potatoes into halves if using new potatoes (or 2-inch chunks for larger potatoes) and the cabbage into 2-inch wedges. Place the potatoes in the middle of the skillet, where they will get the highest heat, and the cabbage wedges around the perimeter. Season to taste with salt and pepper. Lay the sausage on the top of all of it, then cover with a tight-fitting lid.

3. Simmer for 15 to 20 minutes, until the potatoes are tender, checking halfway through the cook time and adding a bit of water or more broth as needed.

4. I serve this with butter so my boys can make mashed potatoes on their plates, which is probably uncouth, but that's a glimpse into my circus!

BREAKFAST-FOR-DINNER BURRITOS

Olive oil

2 cups cooked potato chunks (see page 67), saved forward, cut into 1-inch pieces

Seasoned salt (or table salt)

Ground black pepper

2 cups smoked sausage chunks (see page 67), saved forward, cut into 1-inch chunks

1 tablespoon butter

One dozen eggs, whisked

1 cup shredded cheddar cheese, or your favorite

Corn or flour tortillas—as many as you need!

Salsa, for serving

The pan-fried potatoes in these burritos add flavor, and they're a help to the budget as well. It took me many years to figure out how to make delicious fried potatoes; mine always seemed to burn on the outside before cooking in the middle. The secret? Cook them in advance! Pan-frying already cooked potatoes gives them that crusty goodness.

This dish pairs well with Frozen Fruit Cups (see page 275) if you have a stash in the freezer!

1. Heat a deep, heavy pan (cast iron is excellent!) and add oil to coat the pan's bottom, then heat the oil over medium heat. Add the potatoes and let them cook undisturbed until they start to develop a nice crust, about 5 minutes. Sprinkle with a bit of seasoned salt and pepper. Before they get too browned, lift sections of potatoes with a spatula and flip to brown the other side. When the potatoes are mostly browned, add the sausage and cook until lightly browned, 3 to 5 minutes.

2. Though I am a big fan of not dirtying pans unnecessarily, you'll want to use a nonstick pan to scramble the eggs, unless you have a superpower that I don't have. Heat a large nonstick skillet over medium-high heat and add the butter. Pour in the eggs and start the scrambling process, gently scraping across the bottom of the pan as the eggs cook and swirling to move uncooked egg onto the hot surface, seasoning with seasoned salt and pepper as needed. When the eggs have just begun to set, add the sausage and potatoes and mix them around with the scrambling eggs. Turn off the heat when the eggs are almost set, add the cheese, and let the residual heat melt the cheese.

3. Briefly warm the tortillas in the microwave. Use your favorite method to roll your burritos (or do what I did—go down a rabbit hole on the internet to learn that you've been doing it all wrong!). Or eat tortilla-less to save carbs. Do I need to mention salsa? It's a must, of course.

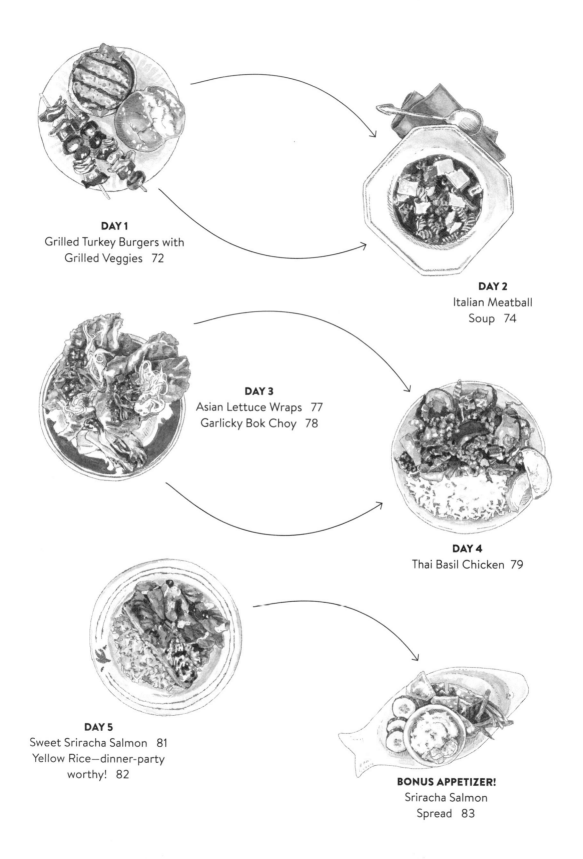

DAY 1
Grilled Turkey Burgers with
Grilled Veggies 72

DAY 2
Italian Meatball
Soup 74

DAY 3
Asian Lettuce Wraps 77
Garlicky Bok Choy 78

DAY 4
Thai Basil Chicken 79

DAY 5
Sweet Sriracha Salmon 81
Yellow Rice—dinner-party
worthy! 82

BONUS APPETIZER!
Sriracha Salmon
Spread 83

WEEK 5
Get a Grip Week

If you're like me, you can find many opportunities in the day to pack on the pounds. Every so often, I need a reset, a week of eating virtuously—a "Get a Grip" week. This week's menu is a bit lighter and less caloric, with plenty of vegetables. It's just as tasty, though, so be not afraid!

GRILLED TURKEY BURGERS with GRILLED VEGGIES

TURKEY BURGERS

2 pounds lean ground turkey

⅔ cup grated zucchini (a box grater is fast and easy)

½ cup grated Parmesan cheese

2 tablespoons Worcestershire sauce

¼ cup ketchup

2 teaspoons mustard

1½ teaspoons table salt

1 teaspoon ground black pepper

Hamburger buns and your favorite burger accompaniments, for serving (or eat bun-less or wrapped with lettuce instead)

SAUCE

½ cup ketchup

2 teaspoons mustard

I originally conceived this recipe as individual meatloaves cooked in the oven, but then I just decided to throw them on the grill one night, which saved me some cleanup time. Two pounds of meat may seem like too much for your family, but you'll be saving forward the leftovers to the next night's soup.

Shhh . . . don't tell anyone, but you've sneaked zucchini into their burgers!

1. Preheat the grill to medium-high. If you plan on using bamboo skewers for your veggies, soak them in water while the grill is preheating.

2. To make the burgers, in a large bowl gently combine the turkey, zucchini, Parmesan, Worcestershire, ketchup, mustard, salt, and pepper. Form the mixture into 8 to 10 patties. To make the sauce, in a small bowl combine the ketchup and mustard.

3. Grill the burgers on a medium-hot grill until no longer pink, about 5 minutes per side, basting with the sauce during the last few minutes of cooking.

4. To make the veggies, in a large bowl, toss the veggies with the olive oil, granulated garlic, salt, and pepper.

5. It is easiest to cook the veggies on a grill pan, but you can skewer them or cook them directly on the grill if you don't have one. The important thing is to cook similarly dense vegetables for the same amount of time, placing the firmest, densest vegetables on the grill first. Start checking them after they've cooked for 3 to 5 minutes for grill marks. If not, let them cook a while longer, then flip to the other

GRILLED VEGGIES

1 pound grill-friendly veggies of your choice, cut into 2-inch chunks (my favorites: bell peppers, mushrooms, zucchini, and onions!; a **SAVE-IT-FORWARD** item)

2 teaspoons olive oil

½ teaspoon granulated garlic or seasoning of your choice

½ teaspoon table salt

⅛ teaspoon ground black pepper

LUNCH BITS AND BOBS:

Grilled veggies are a great addition to salads, so you might want to grill some extras to add to your lunch salads this week.

side. The timing will depend on your cooking method and the temperature of your grill. The key is to leave the veggies undisturbed for a while on each side so they have a chance to develop grill marks. (To cook the veggies in the oven, line a sheet pan with foil and spread the veggies on the pan. Roast at 425°F for 20 to 30 minutes, until done to your liking.)

6. Serve the hamburgers on buns with your favorite accompaniments and the grilled veggies on the side.

SAVE IT FORWARD–GRILLED VEGGIES: If you aren't using your leftover veggies for **Lunch Bits and Bobs**, you can add them to Italian Meatball Soup (page 74).

SAVE IT FORWARD—TURKEY BURGERS: Save 2 cups of turkey burgers chopped into small pieces for tomorrow night's Italian Meatball Soup (page 74).

ITALIAN MEATBALL SOUP

4 cups Overnight Chicken Broth (page 268) or other chicken broth

½ medium zucchini, cut into ½-inch quarter-moons

1 cup 1-inch-cut green beans, or frozen mixed veggies

2 cups chopped Grilled Turkey Burgers (page 72), saved forward (see Note)

One 14.5-ounce can tomatoes with basil, garlic, and oregano

Table salt and ground black pepper

1 cup dried pasta of your choice (I used rotini)

Leftover veggies from last night's grilled veggies (see page 73), saved forward (optional)

This soup comes together in a flash! I used zucchini and fresh green beans, but you can use veggies of your choice. If you have any leftover grilled veggies from last night's meal, throw those in the pot, too. Serve with buttery, crusty bread if you are eschewing the Get a Grip theme, skinny girl.

Place the broth, zucchini, green beans, turkey burgers, and tomatoes in a large saucepan over medium heat and season to taste with salt and pepper. Bring to a simmer and cook for 8 to 10 minutes, until the beans and tomatoes soften a bit. Add the pasta and simmer until cooked according to the package directions. During the last 5 minutes, add the grilled veggies.

NOTE: The turkey burgers will have a little bit of the basted sauce on them, which is fine—it adds to the flavor!

ASIAN LETTUCE WRAPS

Thin rice noodles
(optional)

2 pounds ground chicken
(or turkey would work)

8 garlic cloves, minced
(see Note)

1 tablespoon grated fresh
ginger (see Note)

½ cup low-sodium soy
sauce, plus more to taste

¼ cup lightly packed
brown sugar

½ teaspoon crushed red
pepper flakes

3 green onions, thinly
sliced

One 8-ounce can water
chestnuts, roughly
chopped

Romaine or butter lettuce
leaves, for serving

I love Asian lettuce wraps from restaurants, but have you ever looked at the nutritional numbers? Terrifying! This version is so simple to make that you may never order the take-out version again. Your pants will thank me. You're welcome, pants. Serve with Garlicky Bok Choy (page 78).

1. If using rice noodles, cook according to the package directions and drain.

2. In a large nonstick skillet over medium heat, brown the chicken, breaking it up as you cook, about 5 minutes. Drain most of the liquid from the pan. Add the garlic and ginger and cook until fragrant, about 1 minute. Add the soy sauce, brown sugar, red pepper flakes, green onions, and water chestnuts and cook for 10 minutes, until the liquid cooks down and the flavors meld.

3. Serve the meat mixture in the lettuce wrap boats with a layer of rice noodles and additional soy sauce if desired. (Without the rice noodles, this is a low-carb delight!)

NOTE ON GARLIC AND GINGER: I am usually a fan of garlic in a jar and frozen ginger cubes, but in this recipe, the garlic and ginger are the star players, and I recommend using fresh if possible.

SAVE IT FORWARD—CHICKEN: Reserve 2 cups of the cooked chicken mixture for Thai Basil Chicken (page 79).

GARLICKY BOK CHOY

1 tablespoon olive oil

3 garlic cloves, minced

1 teaspoon grated fresh ginger

1 pound bok choy, sliced (see Note)

½ cup Overnight Chicken Broth (page 268) or other chicken broth

1 tablespoon soy sauce

2 teaspoons sesame oil (optional)

1. Heat a large skillet over medium-high heat. Heat the olive oil, add the garlic and ginger, and cook for 1 to 2 minutes, until fragrant. Add the bok choy and cook until golden brown on each side, using tongs to turn it. Don't be afraid to let it cook on each side until it caramelizes a bit.

2. Add the chicken broth and soy sauce to the pan and simmer until all the broth cooks off. If the bok choy is not quite tender enough, add a small amount of water and cook a bit longer.

3. Drizzle with the sesame oil, if using, and serve.

NOTE ON BOK CHOY: You can use baby or regular bok choy. For either size, trim the root end and wilted leaves; you may also need to discard outer leaves if they are not in good shape. Bok choy often hides dirt, so rinse well (or even soak for a while in water). Cut baby bok choy in half lengthwise and regular bok choy into quarters lengthwise.

SAVE IT FORWARD—BOK CHOY: If you have leftover bok choy, save it to add to tomorrow's Thai Basil Chicken (page 79).

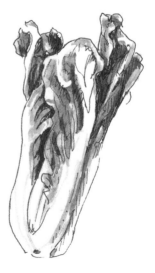

THAI BASIL CHICKEN

2 cups cut-up veggies, such as sliced red bell peppers and green beans

Garlicky Bok Choy (page 78), saved forward, sliced

One 13.5-ounce can coconut milk (I use full fat for maximum flavor, but you can use the light version)

1 to 2 tablespoons red curry paste, depending on your heat tolerance

2 cups cooked chicken from Asian Lettuce Wraps (page 77), saved forward

5 to 7 fresh basil leaves (see Note), sliced into thin strips

Cooked jasmine or white rice, for serving

NOTE ON FRESH BASIL:
I often buy a small basil plant instead of a plastic carton of basil leaves from the produce aisle. It's about the same price, and sometimes I actually get around to planting it. Also, instead of using a knife, I use kitchen scissors to snip the leaves into thin strips.

You'll most often find this recipe cooked with chunks of chicken breast but using cooked ground chicken from last night's Asian Lettuce Wraps makes a quick and tasty save-it-forward shortcut! Fresh pineapple is a lovely accompaniment and makes this a full meal.

1. Add a few tablespoons of water to a deep pan and heat over medium-high heat until simmering. Add the veggies (and leftover bok choy, if using) and flash-cook them until tender, tossing frequently and adding water as needed.

2. Add the coconut milk and whisk in the curry paste. Add the chicken mixture, cover, and simmer, stirring often, until heated through, 5 to 7 minutes.

3. Add the basil right before serving, reserving a bit to sprinkle on top for a pretty garnish. Serve over rice.

SWEET SRIRACHA SALMON

2 pounds salmon fillets

⅓ packed cup brown sugar

1 to 3 tablespoons sriracha, depending on your heat tolerance

1½ teaspoons chili powder

1½ teaspoons table salt

Could I convince you to have a simple dinner party? I promise this dish will be a hit, and it requires minimal effort. Pair with Yellow Rice (page 82) and a pretty salad and you will be guest-ready!

1. Preheat the oven to 400°F and line a sheet pan with foil.

2. Place the salmon on the sheet pan. In a small bowl, combine the brown sugar, sriracha, chili powder, and salt. Slather the fillets with the sriracha mixture.

3. Bake for 12 to 15 minutes, or even longer if your fillets are extra thick. The salmon is cooked to my liking when it easily flakes, though some folks like it less cooked and not fully opaque!

SAVE IT FORWARD—SALMON: If you have leftover salmon, save it for a quick appetizer to accompany a glass of wine over the weekend! See the Sriracha Salmon Spread on page 83.

YELLOW RICE

One 7-ounce box packaged yellow rice, such as Zatarain's

⅓ cup mayonnaise

¾ teaspoon mustard, or to taste

¼ to 1 teaspoon curry powder, to taste

I consider this a bit of a cheat because I start with packaged yellow rice. But I fancy it up with a trick I learned from chef Tiffany Poe, my friend and culinary guru. You may want to double the recipe if you have a dinner party—people love this dish!

Make the rice according to package directions using a nonstick saucepan if you have it. Plop the mayo into the rice, then add the mustard and curry powder and stir to combine. Taste and adjust the flavors to your liking; you may want to add more mustard or curry powder.

SRIRACHA SALMON SPREAD

½ pound Sweet Sriracha Salmon (page 81), saved forward

4 ounces cream cheese, softened briefly in the microwave

2 tablespoons sour cream

2 tablespoons lemon juice

Sriracha (optional; I use about 3 tablespoons)

Table salt

If you have any leftover salmon, treat yourself to a glass of wine accompanied by this spread and some toasty crackers or bread (or veggies if you are still feeling virtuous at the end of Get a Grip Week). This recipe makes a relatively large quantity, but since a small amount of this spread packs quite a punch of flavor, you may want to halve it and use any remaining salmon to top a salad.

1. In the bowl of a mixer or food processor, combine the salmon, cream cheese, sour cream, lemon juice, sriracha, and ½ teaspoon salt. Taste the mixture and adjust the seasonings.

2. Serve or refrigerate, covered, until you are ready to serve.

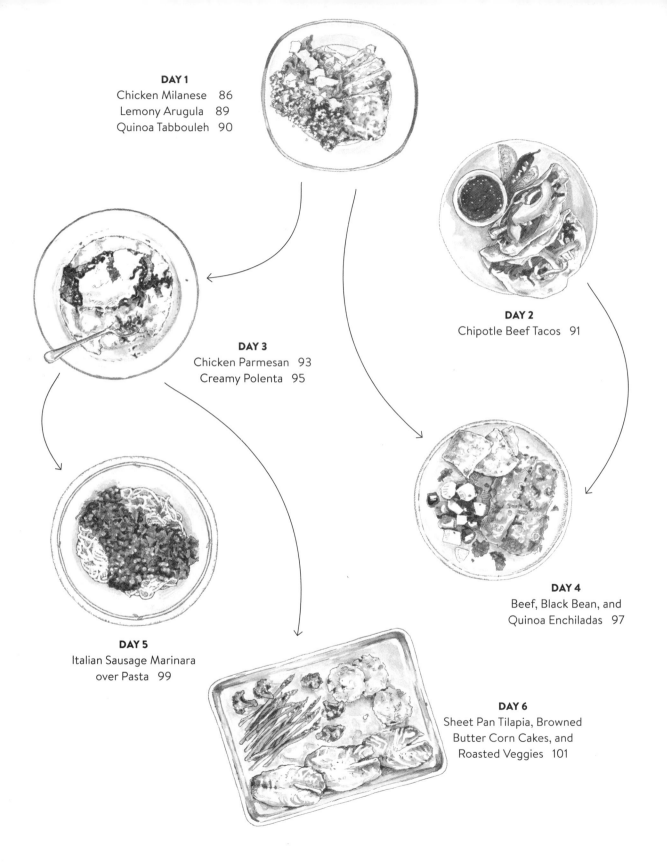

Ancient Grains Week

Though my men are entirely too carnivorous to eat a solely plant-based diet, I like to slip in some unfamiliar grains and inspire (coerce?) them to broaden their culinary horizons. The week starts with man-pleasing chicken (fried!) and beef (tacos!) so that they are lulled into thinking that life is normal, then I surreptitiously slip in some quinoa and polenta—a culinary bait and switch.

CHICKEN MILANESE

6 chicken breasts (a **SAVE-IT-FORWARD** item; see Note)

1 cup flour (gluten-free is fine!)

1 teaspoon table salt, plus more to taste

1 teaspoon ground black pepper, plus more to taste

3 eggs, whisked

2 cups dry bread crumbs or panko (I use Italian-seasoned gluten-free panko)

1 cup shredded Parmesan, plus more for serving if desired

3 tablespoons olive oil

3 tablespoons butter

If you're feeding a houseful of men, you can dub this "fried chicken," so you don't arouse suspicion that you're serving them something weird. I rarely fry anything, which is likely a remnant of coming of age in the era of low-fat dieting. I have since made my peace with (healthy) fats, but I still rarely bother—it's a bit of a process, and as I'm sure you've noticed by now, I like to keep things simple. Though this recipe is a bit more labor-intensive, it's justifiable: (1) it's a weekend meal; (2) it's a twofer, since it becomes Chicken Parm later in the week; and (3) your family (and you) will be insanely happy with this deliciously fried delight of a meal.

TIMING NOTE: Pair this dish with the Lemony Arugula (page 89) and Quinoa Tabbouleh (page 90) recipes that follow. I find that the chicken frying process is all-consuming, so I start the quinoa first.

1. Preheat the oven to 250°F and cover a sheet pan with foil.

2. Pound the chicken breasts to ½-inch thickness using a meat pounder, the flat side of a mallet, or anything heavy (a rolling pin, a can). To protect yourself from flying bits of chicken, put the chicken inside a gallon plastic bag or even between the sides of a folded silicone baking mat.

3. Prepare three plates, one with each of these ingredients: the flour, seasoned with the salt and pepper; the eggs; and the bread crumbs mixed with the Parmesan.

4. Bread the chicken in batches, two breasts at a time. Dredge the chicken in the flour, then dip it in the egg, then dredge it in the bread crumb mixture. While one batch is frying, I dredge only the next two breasts; I find that the breading falls off if you dredge all the chicken before you start frying.

5. In a heavy pan (I use cast iron) over medium-low heat, heat 1 tablespoon of the olive oil and 1 tablespoon of the butter. Add the first two breasts and leave them undisturbed until golden brown on the bottom (2 to 3 minutes), then use tongs to flip them to the other side. Cook for 2 to 3 minutes, until the crust is golden brown and the chicken is cooked throughout.

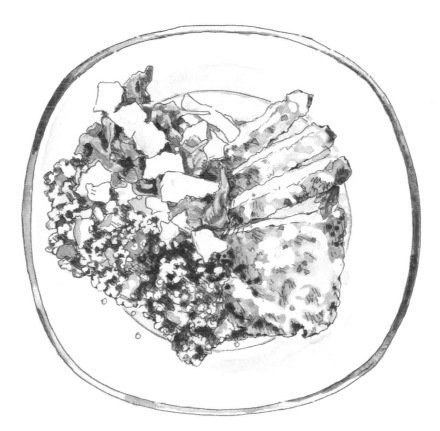

6. Place the breasts on the foil-lined sheet pan and set it in the oven to keep warm. Repeat steps 4 and 5 to bread and cook the rest of the chicken. You will likely need to add 1 tablespoon each of oil and butter between batches. For the first batch of chicken, do not worry if the breasts are still lightly pink after frying since they will be in the warm oven longest and will continue to cook a bit.

7. To serve, cut the breasts in half and place them on plates. Sprinkle with shredded Parmesan.

NOTE ON SERVING SIZE: When you pound a chicken breast, it spreads out quite a bit, and one breast could serve two people with an average appetite (which is what I have calculated for this recipe). However, if you're cooking for extra-hungry people, they might eat an entire breast (or more?), so you might want to cook more. If so, add some more flour, another egg, and more panko accordingly.

SAVE IT FORWARD—CHICKEN: Save enough cooked chicken for Chicken Parmesan (page 93).

LEMONY ARUGULA

4 cups arugula

Juice of ½ lemon

1 tablespoon olive oil

½ to 1 teaspoon kosher salt, or less if using table salt

Parmesan, shredded or shaved, for serving

Serve alongside (or on top of!) the Chicken Milanese (page 86).

Place the arugula in a bowl, drizzle it with the lemon juice and olive oil, sprinkle on the kosher salt, toss to combine, then sprinkle with Parmesan.

QUINOA TABBOULEH

1 cup uncooked quinoa (a
SAVE-IT-FORWARD item)

1 large cucumber, peeled
and medium diced

2 Roma tomatoes, diced

1 cup finely chopped fresh
flat-leaf parsley

2 green onions, thinly
sliced

1 garlic clove, minced

Juice of ½ lemon

2 tablespoons olive oil

½ to ¾ teaspoon table salt

This lemony tabbouleh is a fitting side dish to a fried main dish like Chicken Milanese (page 86); it's full of healthy vegetables and it's not overly starchy and caloric. Though technically quinoa is a seed, it's high in protein, so you can feel more virtuous when eating it, if that kind of virtue is important to you.

1. To prepare the quinoa, rinse it well in cold water, then rinse again, and drain in a fine-mesh strainer. If you have time, you can even soak it a bit before rinsing. Quinoa sometimes gets a bad rap for bitterness but rinsing well solves the problem.

2. Combine the quinoa and 2 cups of water in a small saucepan and bring to a boil over medium-high heat. Cover, reduce the heat, and simmer gently until the water is absorbed, 10 to 15 minutes. Some recipes suggest 20 minutes, but it never takes that long for me. The quinoa is fully cooked when the seeds burst and reveal the cutest little curlicue tail.

3. In a large bowl, combine 2 cups of the cooked quinoa with the cucumber, tomatoes, parsley, green onions, and garlic. Pour in the lemon juice and olive oil and toss. Add salt to taste and toss again.

SAVE IT FORWARD—QUINOA: Reserve 1 cup of cooked quinoa for Beef, Black Bean, and Quinoa Enchiladas (page 97).

CHIPOTLE BEEF TACOS

SEASONING MIX

1 to 3 tablespoons sauce from a can of chipotle chiles in adobo

2 tablespoons chili powder

2 teaspoons ground cumin

2 teaspoons brown sugar

1 teaspoon oregano

2 teaspoons table salt

TACOS

One 3- to 4-pound chuck roast (a bone-in roast adds flavor, but Is often hard to find; a **SAVE-IT-FORWARD** Item)

1 cup Overnight Chicken Broth (page 268) or other chicken broth (or chicken base and water to make 1 cup)

Taco fixins, for serving: shredded cheese, sliced or diced avocado, shredded lettuce, diced tomato, sour cream

Tortillas, for serving

Though I'm a fan of ground beef tacos, these tacos made with a slow-cooked chuck roast are intensely flavored and hold up well for a save-it-forward meal later in the week. Here in Oklahoma, we are accustomed to the heat of chipotles, and I love the smoky flavor, but if you're not in love with spicy foods, use a smaller amount of adobo sauce (or skip it entirely, though that would be a shame!).

LUNCH BITS
AND BOBS:

If you have any extra leftover beef, it makes terrific quesadillas for a quick lunch. If your lunch hour means "lunch thirty minutes," you can prepare the quesadillas the night before and warm them in the microwave.

1. Combine the adobo sauce, chili powder, cumin, brown sugar, oregano, and salt in a small bowl and then rub it all over the chuck roast.

2. Pour the chicken broth into a slow cooker and set the seasoned roast inside. Cook on low for 6 to 8 hours or on high for 4 to 6 hours, until the meat shreds easily with a fork. Shred the meat, removing the fat, and place it back into the juices in the cooker. Set the cooker to warm.

3. Prep your favorite taco fixins and warm the tortillas by wrapping them in a damp paper towel and microwaving for 30 seconds, or until warm and pliable.

4. Serve the beef in the tortillas and let everyone top them as desired.

SAVE IT FORWARD—BEEF: Reserve 1 cup of the beef for Beef, Black Bean, and Quinoa Enchiladas (page 97).

CHICKEN PARMESAN over CREAMY POLENTA

Cooking spray

Cooked breaded cutlets from Chicken Milanese (page 86), saved forward, as many as needed to serve your diners

Creamy Polenta (page 95)

Simple Slow Cooker Marinara (see **Advance Prep on page 94**; a **SAVE-IT-FORWARD** item) or jarred marinara

One 8-ounce ball fresh mozzarella, cut into thinnish slices—1 per piece of chicken

Shredded Parmesan, for serving

Day 1's breaded chicken magically transforms into Chicken Parmesan tonight, and tonight's leftover Creamy Polenta (page 95) will turn into corn cakes (page 101) later in the week. You're not sacrificing flavor with all this efficiency, though: every expedited meal will delight your diners!

ADVANCE PREP

If you're making Simple Slow Cooker Marinara (page 270), you can start it in the morning or at lunchtime in the slow cooker. Or use jarred sauce—you'll get no judgment from me!

1. Preheat the oven to 300°F. Line a sheet pan with foil and spray it with cooking spray.

2. Place the cooked breaded chicken on the foil-lined pan and warm it in the oven for 30 minutes while you prepare the polenta.

3. If you don't have a batch of marinara in the slow cooker, warm the jarred marinara sauce in the microwave or in a saucepan over low heat.

4. Place a slice of mozzarella on each cutlet. Turn the oven to broil and return the pan to the top or an upper rack in the oven. Broil until the cheese is melted and bubbly, watching carefully to ensure the chicken doesn't burn—it will take only a minute or two.

5. Assemble your creation: Place some polenta in the middle of a plate or shallow bowl, nestle the cheesy chicken cutlet on top, and spoon the marinara sauce all over. Sprinkle with Parmesan and serve.

CREAMY POLENTA

3 cups broth (or milk)

1½ teaspoons table salt

1½ cups corn grits or cornmeal

¾ cup grated Parmesan or fontina cheese, or cheese of your choice

The internet has a lot of opinions about polenta, aka "grits"— particularly when Southerners and Italians weigh in! I use "Corn Grits, also known as Polenta" from Bob's Red Mill and cook them for 20(ish) minutes. My recipe tester, Brandi, tried making polenta with plain old cornmeal and the five-minute "quick grits" method and said it worked just fine. Some folks use water only; some use broth only (or broth and water); I use water and a little milk, and add a little cheese at the end for an incredibly creamy dish. Even if you think you're a grits hater, give them a try!

If you start your polenta right before the chicken, the timing will be perfect. If you get a late start, just follow the "quick grits" directions on a package of cornmeal and add some cheese at the end.

1. In a large heavy-bottomed saucepan over medium-high heat, bring 3 cups of water, the milk or broth (a total of 6 cups of liquid), and the salt to a boil. Add the grits or cornmeal slowly, whisking to prevent clumping, and turn the heat to low. Cook for 15 to 20 minutes, depending on your stove's definition of low, until the grits are creamy and all the liquid has been absorbed. If the water absorbs too fast, and the grains are "crunchy," add a bit more water and cook on low until the liquid is absorbed, repeating that process, if necessary. You will need to stir fairly often; if you happen to burn the grits on the bottom, don't scrape! It will just bring up all the burnt stuff into your polenta. Just pretend it didn't happen and continue stirring the polenta above the burnt stuff.

2. Add the cheese and stir to combine.

3. Serve in a bowl or on a plate.

SAVE IT FORWARD: Reserve leftover polenta for Browned Butter Corn Cakes (see page 101). Spread the polenta in a ½- to 1-inch layer in a sheet pan or casserole dish, cover with foil or plastic wrap, and refrigerate.

BEEF, BLACK BEAN, AND QUINOA ENCHILADAS

Cooking spray

1 cup shredded beef from Chipotle Beef Tacos (page 91), saved forward

One 15.5-ounce can black beans, drained but not rinsed

1 cup cooked quinoa (see page 90), saved forward

2 cups baby spinach (optional, but adds some healthy veggies!)

One 10-ounce can red enchilada sauce

2½ cups grated cheese, such as cheddar or pepper Jack

Twelve 5-inch corn tortillas

Just add fruit, chips, and salsa for a satisfying and delicious meal. I make a quick fruit salad from chunks of pineapple, papaya, and mango sprinkled with chili powder and salt and with a squeeze of lime (my knockoff of Trader Joe's Chili Lime Seasoning, which is a fantastic shortcut item).

1. Preheat the oven to 350°F and spray a 9 x 13-inch pan with cooking spray.

2. In a bowl, mix the beef, beans, quinoa, spinach, ½ cup of the enchilada sauce, and ½ cup of the grated cheese.

3. Wrap the tortillas in a damp paper towel and microwave for 30 seconds, until warm and pliable.

4. Spread ½ cup of the enchilada sauce on the bottom of the pan.

5. To make an enchilada, place a scant ¼ cup of the meat mixture onto a tortilla, roll it like a cigar, and place it seam side down in the pan. Repeat to make the rest of the enchiladas. They may tear and not stay in a perfect roll, but it won't matter once you cover them with cheese.

6. Cover the enchiladas with the rest of the enchilada sauce and sprinkle with the remaining 2 cups of cheese

7. Bake for 20 minutes, until the cheese is melted and the sauce is bubbling.

ITALIAN SAUSAGE MARINARA OVER PASTA

¾ cup per person Simple Slow Cooker Marinara (page 270), saved forward, or jarred marinara

Italian sausage links, sweet or hot

2 to 3 ounces uncooked pasta per person (I use rigatoni)

Grated Parmesan, for serving

I am tempted to apologize for this recipe, which is not a recipe at all but just an assemblage of ingredients. Instead of apologizing, though, I decided to congratulate myself that the save-it-forward method lets you have a healthy home-cooked meal with almost no prep. In keeping with the ease of this meal, I add a Caesar salad kit from the produce aisle and congratulate myself a second time for staying out of the drive-through lane. (Can you tell I like to congratulate myself whenever possible?!)

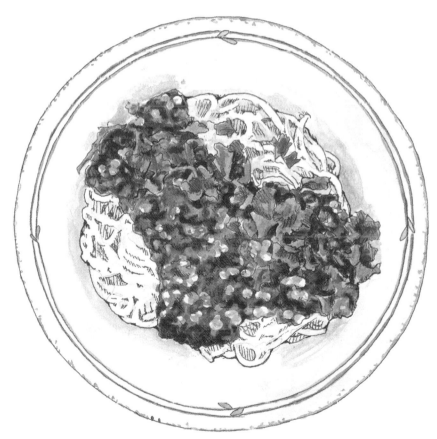

**LUNCH BITS
AND BOBS:**
*Leftover Italian
sausage and
marinara would
make a fantastic
sausage sub, topped
with provolone and
broiled. Or spice up
scrambled eggs with
sliced Italian sausage
(I'd rinse off the excess
marinara, but maybe
you'd love it!).*

1. Place the marinara and Italian sausage in the slow cooker. Cook on high for 4 to 6 hours or low for 6 to 8 hours, until the sausage is cooked through. You can even use frozen sausage and it will be cooked by dinnertime.

2. Cook the pasta according to the package directions and serve with the marinara and sausage, and top with a sprinkle of Parmesan.

SHEET PAN TILAPIA, BROWNED BUTTER CORN CAKES, AND ROASTED VEGGIES

1 pound roastable vegetables of your choice (I like asparagus and broccoli)

2 tablespoons olive oil

Table salt and ground black pepper, to taste

Cooking spray

6 tilapia fillets, thawed

Your favorite seasoning blend for the tilapia (Cajun, Italian, Greek, Peloponnesian—whatever!)

Creamy Polenta (page 95), saved forward

4 tablespoons (½ stick) butter

1 garlic clove, minced

When you've completely forgotten to plan for dinner, tilapia is your BFF (best fish friend). Since I live in the middle of nowhere, the only tilapia I am familiar with is frozen in single-fillet packaging. (Do my urban friends have fish markets with fresh tilapia? I must know the answer to this!) You can pull those babies out of the freezer shortly before dinner, plunk them in the sink and run water over them in their packaging, and they will be ready to cook in minutes. The best practice would be to thaw them in the fridge overnight, but whatever you do, don't cook them from a frozen state.

An exciting twist to this meal is the Browned Butter Corn Cakes. You know the leftover polenta you saved forward on Day 3? It's been waiting for you to cut into cakes and bake (with nutty browned butter!) on a sheet pan with your tilapia. I did a side-by-side taste test of pan-fried corn cakes and sheet pan–baked corn cakes and was surprised at the results. I thought the pan-fried would surely win the taste test, but honestly it was too close to call. Given the ease of making the corn cakes on the same sheet pan instead of dirtying another pan, they're a winner! The secret, I think, is the browned butter—don't skip this three-minute step.

1. Preheat the oven to 425°F. Cover two sheet pans with foil for easy cleanup.

2. Prepare the veggies by cutting them into similar-size pieces so that they will cook at about the same rate. Place on one of the sheet pans and toss with the oil, salt, and pepper, keeping the types of vegetables separated so that if

LUNCH BITS AND BOBS:
Leftover tilapia makes excellent fish tacos!

one veggie is cooking faster than another, you can remove it from the pan early. Roast the veggies for about 20 minutes, depending on the vegetables, until cooked to your liking.

3. Meanwhile, spray the other sheet pan with cooking spray and place the tilapia fillets on it. Since tilapia is a mild fish, a lot of the flavor will come from the seasoning, but fillets are thin, so don't get too aggressive. I sprinkle one side with a light layer of seasoning, if that helps.

4. Cut the polenta into cakes in whatever size and shape you like; the important part is that they be no more than ½ inch to 1 inch thick. Scoring the entire pan into rectangles or squares avoids any waste, but feel free to use cookie cutters to make circles or koala bears—whatever you like! Use a spatula to remove the cakes to the prepared sheet pan with the tilapia, leaving at least an inch of space between them.

5. To brown the butter, melt it in a small saucepan over medium-low heat. Cook for 3 to 5 minutes, depending on your pan and stove, whisking periodically at first, then continually when the butter turns golden brown. Add the garlic when the butter begins to brown and cook for 30 seconds, whisking constantly. Remove from the heat.

6. Stir the butter, then pour it over the tilapia and corn cakes. Bake for 11 minutes, or until the tilapia flakes with a fork.

7. Check the veggies when you put the tilapia in the oven; they will likely need to cook for the entire time that the tilapia cooks, but watch and take them out when they are done to your liking. Don't be afraid to let your veggies get really browned!

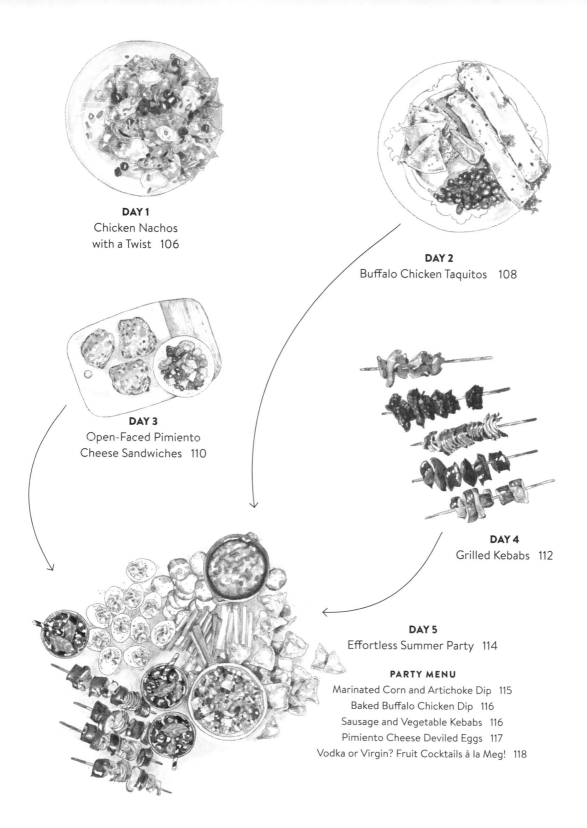

DAY 1
Chicken Nachos
with a Twist 106

DAY 2
Buffalo Chicken Taquitos 108

DAY 3
Open-Faced Pimiento
Cheese Sandwiches 110

DAY 4
Grilled Kebabs 112

DAY 5
Effortless Summer Party 114

PARTY MENU
Marinated Corn and Artichoke Dip 115
Baked Buffalo Chicken Dip 116
Sausage and Vegetable Kebabs 116
Pimiento Cheese Deviled Eggs 117
Vodka or Virgin? Fruit Cocktails à la Meg! 118

Effortless Party Week

At the end of the week, you're going to host a party! Don't argue with me about this. You are. It's going to be so effortless that you won't even think of it as a party. Let's just call it a get-together to lower your blood pressure. I've made the plans, and all you have to do is invite your people—just six of them! Family? Coworkers? The strangers-who-could-become-friends next to you at the nail salon? You know that old saying "If you want a friend, be a friend"? It's true!

Here's the game plan: every meal you cook for your family this week will be super easy, so you'll have extra time for a bit of house prep (which does not mean re-tiling your bathroom; it means swishing your toilet with a bit of cleaner). Several components in this week's meals will be repurposed for the party, so you'll have minimal cooking to do on the night of the get-together.

I've planned only the main dishes because I want this week to be effortless. This week is the time to bust out those canned vegetables in your pantry for the side dishes for your meal—black beans, green beans, corn, whatever. Or make a quick green or fruit salad. Keep it simple!

ADVANCE PREP

CHICKEN: You can cook Indispensable Mexican Chicken (page 267) for the nachos and taquitos in the slow cooker over the weekend or on the same day as your meal. You might have a bit of chicken left over, but it will make a lovely topping for a salad—think **Lunch Bits and Bobs!**

CHEESE: A couple of the dishes this week call for grated cheese, and I plead with you to grate it fresh. For the sake of efficiency, you can grate it all on the weekend and store it in an airtight container. I would grate 2 pounds of cheese: 1½ pounds of cheddar (I like sharp!) and ½ pound of something more exotic for the pimiento cheese—a pepper Jack is nice.

CHICKEN NACHOS WITH A TWIST

1 head cauliflower

2 tablespoons olive oil

Table salt and ground black pepper

2 to 3 cups Indispensable Mexican Chicken (page 267; saved forward)

2 tablespoons sauce from a can of chipotle chiles in adobo (use just the sauce or include some of the chiles, chopped)

¾ cup sour cream

Milk

Half a 12-ounce bag of tortilla chips

One 2.25-ounce can sliced black olives (or two if you are olive-obsessed like me)

3 green onions, thinly sliced (or ½ cup red onion slivers)

2 cups grated cheese, such as cheddar or pepper Jack

¾ cup finely diced tomatoes

You know how I'm always trying to work more vegetables into my diet? I'm at it again with this recipe with some roasted cauliflower. When roasted, cauliflower is virtually the same color as a tortilla chip, so I thought my family would never notice my camouflage subterfuge. Well, they did notice—but they thought it was a tasty twist! The chipotle sour cream drizzle at the end makes these special. If you aren't feeling adventuresome, I won't be overly grumpy if you skip the cauliflower (but promise me that you'll try it at least once!).

LUNCH BITS AND BOBS:

If you have leftovers, remove the chips and save everything else for a quick lunch as a topper for salad or rice or wrapped in a tortilla with additional chipotle sour cream sauce.

1. Preheat the oven to 425°F. Cover a sheet pan with foil.

2. Prepping the cauliflower takes longer than one might expect, so start making this meal before you get really hungry. Cut off the stem of the cauliflower, then slice the head into flat ½-inch-thick slabs. Cut out most of the tough core but keep some of it intact to hold the slabs together. Place the cauliflower on the prepared sheet pan, drizzle with the oil, and gently toss to coat both sides of the cauliflower. Season with salt and pepper.

3. Roast the cauliflower until nicely browned, 40 minutes or even longer, but start checking at 30 minutes.

4. Meanwhile, if you made the chicken ahead, warm it in the microwave.

5. In a medium bowl, combine the chipotle adobo sauce and sour cream. Thin it with milk until drizzleable (is that a word?). Add salt to taste.

6. When cauliflower is nicely browned, remove it from the oven and lift the foil off the pan to set the cauliflower aside. Spread the tortilla chips on the pan. Remove the cauliflower from the foil and arrange it on top of the chips. Top with the chicken, olives, green onions, and cheese and broil until the cheese is melted and bubbly.

7. Sprinkle the tomatoes over the nachos and drizzle them with chipotle sauce. Serve, and let me know what your family thinks!

BUFFALO CHICKEN TAQUITOS

4 cups Indispensable Mexican Chicken (page 267; saved forward)

Two 8-ounce packages cream cheese (I use reduced-fat), at room temperature

2 teaspoons garlic powder

2 cups grated cheddar cheese

1 cup crumbled feta cheese

1 cup Frank's RedHot Original Cayenne Pepper Sauce

Twelve 6½-inch flour tortillas (see Note on page 109)

Cooking spray

Salsa, for serving (optional)

This recipe will make enough filling for taquitos tonight and a party dip for this weekend—hurray! If you're being stubborn and refusing to host a party this weekend, halve this recipe and it will make enough for just the taquitos.

Round out the meal with simple side dishes like black beans (from a can, my friend) and chips and salsa—remember, you're saving your energy for your party this weekend!

1. Preheat the oven to 400°F and line a sheet pan with foil.

2. In a large microwave-safe bowl, combine the chicken, cream cheese, garlic powder, cheddar, feta, and Frank's RedHot. Microwave on low power, a couple of minutes at a time, stirring frequently until the cheese and cream cheese are melted. You can also put the ingredients in a slow cooker on low for a couple of hours.

3. Lay a tortilla flat and place a scant ¼ cup of filling in a line down the middle. Roll it up like a cigar and place it seam side down on the prepared sheet pan. Repeat to make the rest of the taquitos. Spray lightly with cooking spray.

4. Bake for 15 minutes, flip the taquitos, spray with cooking spray, and bake for 8 to 10 minutes more, until crispy. If you want them a bit crispier, broil them for a few minutes, watching them closely.

5. Let the taquitos sit for 5 to 10 minutes before serving. Serve with salsa if you like!

NOTE ON TORTILLAS: I tested this with corn tortillas, but they don't hold a taquito shape as well as flour tortillas. To make this dish gluten-free, I would recommend either just eating it as a dip with corn tortilla chips or making quesadillas with corn tortillas.

SAVE IT FORWARD—FILLING: The leftover filling will be used as a dip for your *partay* at the end of the week (see page 116); freeze it in your prettiest freezer-to-oven baking dish to make sure it stays fresh.

OPEN-FACED PIMIENTO CHEESE SANDWICHES

Bread slices (see Note on page 111), enough to serve each person an open-faced sandwich

1 pound cheese, grated (see Note on page 111)

1 cup mayonnaise (Duke's brand if you can find it!)

¼ to ½ teaspoon cayenne pepper (depending on your heat tolerance)

½ teaspoon sugar

1 teaspoon red wine (or other) vinegar

½ teaspoon smoked or regular paprika (optional but delicious)

One 4-ounce jar diced pimientos, drained

I have been trying for years to re-create my mom's recipe for pimiento cheese, which I failed to ask her for before she passed away. Wahhh—if your mother is still alive and has great recipes, ask her now! I have tweaked and tinkered and finally came up with this version, which matches my childhood memories. Though it is terrific at room temperature with crackers, it's exceptional when broiled and melty. This recipe makes enough for leftovers for your party this week—you're inviting people over, right?! The pimiento cheese will keep for several days, so even if you refuse to have a party, you can make the same quantity and keep it all for yourself (it stays fresh for a long time).

If you pair this meal with a fruit salad, you can cut up extra fruit to make the vodka or virgin fruit cocktails (page 118) for the partay!

1. Preheat the oven to 350°F.

2. Place the bread on a sheet pan and toast it for 10 minutes, or until light brown, turning it after 5 minutes. (Or you can just lightly toast it in a toaster.)

3. In a large bowl, combine the cheese, mayonnaise, cayenne, sugar, vinegar, and paprika, if using. Whisk gently to combine. Add the pimientos to the bowl and stir to combine.

4. Slather the toasts with a layer of pimiento cheese, return them to the sheet pan, and bake for 8 to 10 minutes, until the cheese is melted. For a finishing touch, broil them until browned. Keep a close watch on them so they don't burn!

TO DO TONIGHT:

1. *Start marinating the meat tonight for Grilled Kebabs (page 112), for more tenderness and flavor.*
2. *Cut up fruit and make ahead the virgin or vodka fruit cocktails (see page 118).*
3. *Boil and peel the eggs for Pimiento Cheese Deviled Eggs (page 117).*

NOTE ON BREAD: This sandwich is entirely delicious on good ol' white bread. However, if you put it on crusty, substantial Italian bread, or pretzel buns, or sourdough bread, it becomes guest-worthy.

NOTE ON CHEESE (A MANIFESTO): I have no quarrels with pre-grated cheese in some culinary situations, but this is not the time, friends. You must, must, must grate it yourself. I would suggest that you use sharp cheddar for ½ to ¾ pound of the cheese, then go wild with the other ½ to ¼ pound. Pepper Jack is my favorite, though Swiss or smoked Gouda is delicious, too—the world of cheese is yours! I was inspired to add smoked paprika to this recipe when I stumbled upon a smoked paprika cheese, which added a distinct flavor. You must tell me if you come up with a unique cheese tweak!

SAVE IT FORWARD—PIMIENTO CHEESE: Save ⅓ cup for Pimiento Cheese Deviled Eggs (page 117) for the party.

GRILLED KEBABS

Special tools: bamboo skewers (see Note)

1½ pounds sirloin or eye of round steak, cut into 1½-inch chunks

One recipe Matt's Marinade (page 271); reserve ¼ cup for basting

1 to 2 red onions, cut into chunks

1 to 2 zucchinis, cut into chunks

2 red and/or orange bell peppers, cut into chunks

1 pound good-quality smoked sausage or brats, cut into 1-inch-thick rounds

I've fiddled around with kebabs and figured out that you can grill them on one night and reheat them in the oven right before your party. Best news ever! I've planned for you to grill two types of meat tonight: steak and smoked sausage. The steak is for your family tonight and the sausage is for the party tomorrow. Here's my rationale: the sausage is easier to eat if your gathering will be a stand-up, mingling affair instead of a sit-down dinner (which I recommend—let's keep it casual and relaxed!).

If you'd rather not mess with marinating steak for tonight's meal, and you don't mind eating sausage two nights in a row, feel free to skip the steak and prepare all the kebabs with sausage.

To save money, I suggest a less-expensive cut of beef for these skewers; hopefully you started marinating the beef after last night's dinner, but this morning is okay as well.

Pair this with a simple rice dish and you have a complete meal. (There's no shame in a packaged rice mix, by the way!)

1. The night before or (at the latest) 8 hours before serving, combine the steak chunks with the marinade in a bowl or resealable bag and marinate in the refrigerator. After the meat has marinated, reserve the marinade for basting during grilling.

2. Preheat the grill to medium high.

3. For tonight's dinner, thread chunks of steak, onions, zucchinis, and peppers onto bamboo skewers, putting one type of meat or veg on each skewer so everything cooks evenly. To prep for the party, break other skewers in half and

TO DO TONIGHT:
This is optional, but if you want to have more of your party food prepped ahead of time, you could make the Marinated Corn and Artichoke Dip (page 115) tonight.

mix the sausage and the remaining onions, zucchinis, and peppers on each skewer, so they look pretty (see Note on page 113). They all cook at about the same rate, so it will be fine!

4. Place the skewers on the grill and baste the meat and vegetables with the reserved marinade. Grill until marks develop, then turn to grill the other side and baste again. The steak skewers will take 6 to 7 minutes total, depending on the size of the chunks. If you are a precise sort, you can use a meat thermometer; 140°F will give you medium doneness. Sausage skewers will take less time; you can gauge their doneness by the appearance of grill marks.

5. To serve tonight, take the steak and vegetables off the long skewers and divide them among plates.

NOTE ON SKEWERS: I usually use metal skewers for grilling, but for the party I recommend using bamboo skewers from the dollar store. For the party itself I snap them in half to make cute half-size kebabs—very pretty on a platter (and cost-effective to serve a small amount)!

While you're prepping the veggies, soak the skewers so they will be somewhat flame-resistant. Just add some water to a sheet pan and lay them in. You can use the same pan later to transport the kebabs to the grill—just one pan to wash!

SAVE IT FORWARD—SKEWERS: Place the party skewers in a single layer on a sheet of foil (possibly 2 sheets), then cover with another sheet of foil, rolling and sealing the edges to make a package. Store the package in the fridge and they are ready to pop in the oven before the party.

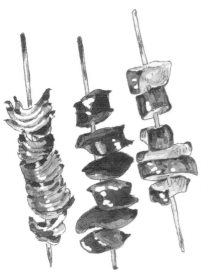

EFFORTLESS SUMMER PARTY

MENU

MARINATED CORN AND ARTICHOKE DIP

BAKED BUFFALO CHICKEN DIP

SAUSAGE AND VEGETABLE KEBABS

PIMIENTO CHEESE DEVILED EGGS

VODKA OR VIRGIN? FRUIT COCKTAILS À LA MEG!

MARINATED CORN AND ARTICHOKE DIP

One 11-ounce can shoepeg corn, drained

One 12-ounce jar marinated artichoke hearts, chopped, but don't drain!

½ cup cherry tomatoes, sliced into quarters

Two-thirds of a 4.25-ounce can black olives, drained and chopped

Small red or orange bell pepper, cut into small dice

1 tablespoon olive oil

1 teaspoon vinegar (I use red wine vinegar)

⅛ teaspoon cayenne pepper

½ teaspoon garlic powder

1 teaspoon table salt

Tortilla chips, for serving

If you are a civilized sort, you will eat this as a salad with a fork. In the Wild West where I live, we play fast and loose with the rules of etiquette and are likely to serve this as a dip with tortilla chips, in the vein of "Texas caviar."

In a pretty serving bowl, combine the corn, artichoke hearts, tomatoes, olives, bell pepper, oil, vinegar, cayenne pepper, garlic powder, and salt and toss well. Refrigerate it if you make it ahead. Serve at room temperature with the tortilla chips. Forks are optional!

BAKED BUFFALO CHICKEN DIP

Filling from Buffalo Chicken Taquitos (page 108), saved forward, frozen or thawed

Tortilla chips, crackers, and/or celery and carrot sticks, for serving

Magically, the taquito filling from earlier in the week becomes a bubbly, cheesy, crowd-pleasing party dip—voilà!

1. Preheat the oven to 350°F.

2. If your filling is in an ovenproof dish, you can pop it in the oven and bake from frozen, though I would allow it to sit on the counter for a while before placing it in the oven to lessen the risk of a cracked dish. If baking from frozen, it will take about an hour to get hot and bubbly. If thawed overnight in the fridge, it will take around 20 minutes. If you need to, you can give it a jump-start in the microwave.

3. Serve with the tortilla chips, crackers, and/or celery and carrot sticks.

SAUSAGE AND VEGETABLE KEBABS

Kebab skewers, saved forward

1. Preheat the oven to 350°F.

2. Heat the foil packet of kebabs in the oven for 15 to 20 minutes, until warmed through.

3. Arrange the mini skewers artistically on a pretty plate and serve!

PIMIENTO CHEESE DEVILED EGGS

10 eggs, hard-boiled, peeled, and halved (see page 18)

⅓ cup pimiento cheese (see page 110), saved forward

¼ cup mayonnaise

⅛ teaspoon cayenne pepper or a splash of your favorite hot sauce

Paprika, for garnish

Deviled eggs have a devilish way of being instantly devoured when plunked on a buffet table; have you noticed this phenomenon? I probably shouldn't have included the additional enticement of pimiento cheese in this recipe, but I want you to be the hostess with the mostest, so I couldn't resist.

TIMING NOTE: It is best to make these on the day of the party so they don't dry out.

1. Pop the yolks out of the hard-boiled eggs and place them in a bowl. Add the pimiento cheese, mayo, and cayenne and mash with a fork until combined.

2. Place a small mound of the filling into the cavity of each egg white half. I prefer to fill only 16 of the egg halves, not the whole 20, so that the filling is more plentiful—and you won't have to fret if one of the egg whites tears. The extra egg white halves can be a little snack for the chef.

3. Sprinkle a bit of paprika on top to add a little color!

VODKA OR VIRGIN? FRUIT COCKTAILS À LA MEG!

SIMPLE SYRUP

½ cup granulated sugar

½ cup water

SPIKED FRUIT COCKTAIL

4 cups (1 quart) vodka (I like citrus vodka!)

6 cups bite-size assorted fruit (such as diced watermelon or nectarines, or whole grapes)

Fresh mint or basil leaves (optional)

Sparkling water (I like Topo Chico because of its extreme fizziness)

We have a family motto about our daughter, Meg (sister to her three brothers): "Meg—she's the best of us!" Not only is she a paragon of virtue, joy, and beauty, she makes a mean cocktail, which I'm delighted to share with you.

It's hard to say how many this will serve because I don't know how rowdy your friends are. This amount would be plenty for my boring pals and me, but if your friends are more fun than mine, adjust the quantity accordingly. If you have any left over, it will last for a good long time in the freezer (well, unless you can't resist it). Also, you may like more or less booziness, so change the proportions to suit your crowd.

You may want to make a double batch of simple syrup and keep it in the fridge. It lasts for months, and you never know when you might need an emergency cocktail!

1. Place the sugar and water in a saucepan and heat over medium heat, stirring until the sugar is dissolved. Let cool before adding to the fruit mixture.

2. Choose a large pitcher that will hold all the ingredients and fit into your freezer. Combine the simple syrup, vodka, and fruit in the pitcher, stir, and set the pitcher in the freezer. To make the drinks, you may need to take the pitcher out of the freezer a bit in advance; the liquid won't freeze solid but will be a bit slushy.

3. If you're using mint or basil, add a few leaves to the bottom of a sturdy cocktail glass and use a muddler (or a spoon) to gently press the leaves until you can smell their aroma (don't muddle them to bits!). To compose a cocktail, I pour in a jigger of the slushy vodka mixture, add a few pieces of fruit, and top off the glass with sparkling water. Stir and serve.

Variation: Virgin Fruit Cocktail

Freeze some bite-size pieces of fruit. Muddle fresh mint or basil in a cocktail glass. Add a few pieces of the frozen fruit and a tablespoon of simple syrup. Top with sparkling water and stir. Adjust the sweetness by adding more simple syrup or sparkling water according to your preference.

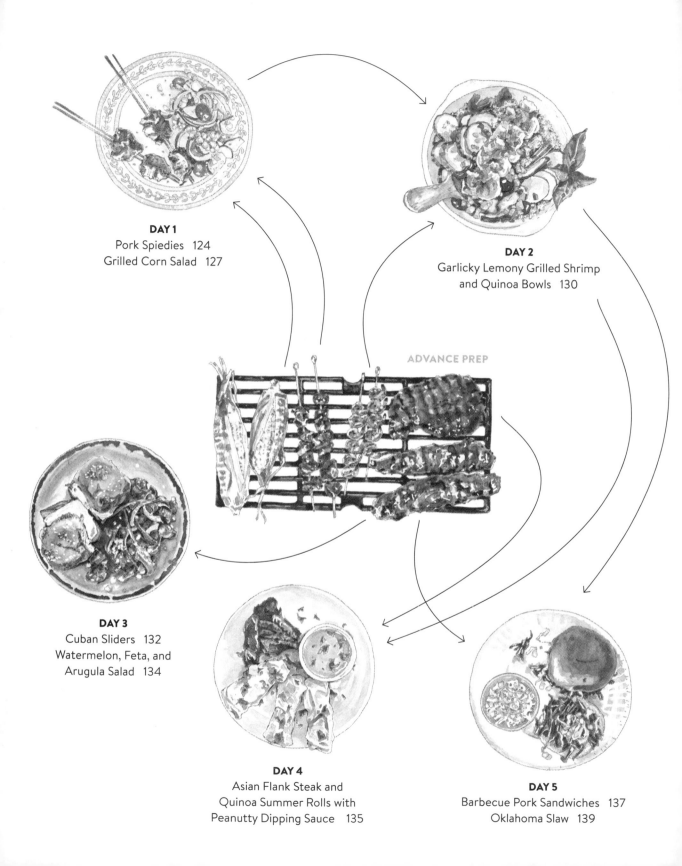

DAY 1
Pork Spiedies 124
Grilled Corn Salad 127

DAY 2
Garlicky Lemony Grilled Shrimp
and Quinoa Bowls 130

ADVANCE PREP

DAY 3
Cuban Sliders 132
Watermelon, Feta, and
Arugula Salad 134

DAY 4
Asian Flank Steak and
Quinoa Summer Rolls with
Peanutty Dipping Sauce 135

DAY 5
Barbecue Pork Sandwiches 137
Oklahoma Slaw 139

Grill Week!

This week we will grill a flank steak, a pork tenderloin, pork kebabs, shrimp, and corn in one fell swoop at the start of the week, and most of these items will become components for other fabulous meals later in the week. You're a meal-prep rock star!

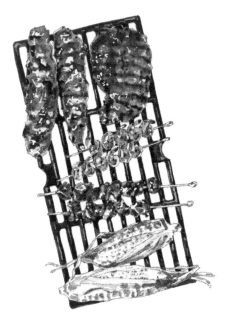

NOTE ON TIMING: The meat and shrimp for the week will be grilled at the same time, but you'll start marinating the spiedies (pork kebabs) and the flank steak the night before grilling (or even sooner) to maximize the flavor. If you want to expedite the barbecued pork meal, you could simmer it in the slow cooker early in the week, freeze it, and reheat it for a quick meal on the day you serve it.

NOTE ON GROCERIES: You'll be using the same fresh ingredients in a few meals so that you won't be left with wasted food. For example, you'll use the slaw mix in the quinoa bowls, the summer rolls, and the Oklahoma Slaw. You'll also have some overlap with fresh herbs in a few recipes, so you'll be using the entire carton of herbs.

NOTE ON MEATS AND QUANTITIES: To help you decide how much meat you need to buy, let me tell you a little about this week's meals. In terms of the pork tenderloin, you'll have one meal of spiedies in which the pork is the star of the show, so I would allow perhaps 4 to 6 ounces per person. You'll need just 2 ounces of meat per sandwich for the Cuban sliders, and for the barbecued pork, I'm estimating 3 ounces per sandwich (or per baked potato, if you choose to serve the pork on a potato rather than a bun). So, allow 9 to 11 ounces of pork per person for the entire week, though YPMMV (Your Pork Mileage May Vary). To sum it up in case that was *waaayyy* too much math for you, you'll likely need to buy two packages of two pork tenderloins each: one for the spiedies and one for the Cubans and pork sandwiches.

Please note that these recipes call for pork *tenderloins*, not a pork loin. The tenderloins are smaller in diameter, so they can be cooked on a grill.

I would allow 3 to 4 ounces of steak per person for the flank steak. The steak will be sliced when served, so you can fan it out on the plate, thus making it look like there's more on each plate, thanks to this culinary sleight of hand.

Before Day 1: Marinade and Dressing Prep

The day or night before the grill-a-thon, you'll do a tad of prep. In a resealable bag, marinate kebab-size pieces of pork tenderloin for the spiedies. While you're at it, you might as well apply the rub to the whole tenderloins for the grilled pork you'll be making ahead and stick the pork in another resealable bag—maximum efficiency, baby! In another bag, marinate the flank steak. Since you're already using olive oil and some other ingredients that overlap with the marinades, make a salad dressing that does double duty as a shrimp marinade. (But don't marinate the shrimp yet: it needs to marinate for only a couple hours at most.)

PORK SPIEDIES

Special tools: metal skewers or bamboo skewers soaked in water

Pork tenderloin, 4 to 6 ounces per person (see page 122 for Note on quantities), cut into kebab-size pieces

½ cup red wine vinegar

Zest and juice of 1 lemon

½ cup olive oil

5 garlic cloves, roughly chopped

1 tablespoon thinly sliced fresh mint leaves

1 tablespoon thinly sliced fresh basil leaves

⅓ cup chopped fresh flat-leaf parsley

1 teaspoon dried oregano

1 bay leaf

2 teaspoons sugar

½ teaspoon crushed red pepper flakes

1 teaspoon table salt

Don't be overwhelmed by the amount of food you'll prepare today (with a little prep the night before). I promise that it's simple, and many of the ingredients overlap. This is the dish you'll actually be eating tonight! Spiedies, a regional New York specialty, are herby, zingy marinated pork kebabs. They're so tasty that an entire festival is named after them. Eat these for tonight's meal since they won't reheat as well as the other choices from your cornucopia of grilled meats. The locals wrap a slice of Italian bread around the meat for a makeshift sandwich. Combined with Grilled Corn Salad (page 127), it's truly festival-worthy!

NOTE: The spiedie marinade is enough for up to 3 pounds of pork.

1. Combine the pork, vinegar, lemon zest and juice, oil, garlic, mint, basil, parsley, oregano, bay leaf, sugar, red pepper flakes, and salt in a resealable plastic bag and marinate overnight in the fridge—or if you aspire to be an upstate New Yorker, 2 to 3 days.

2. Preheat the grill to medium. Place the meat on skewers and grill, turning occasionally, for 10 to 20 minutes, until the meat is light pink inside or an instant-read thermometer registers 145°F. The cooking time depends on the grill temp and the size of the meat chunks.

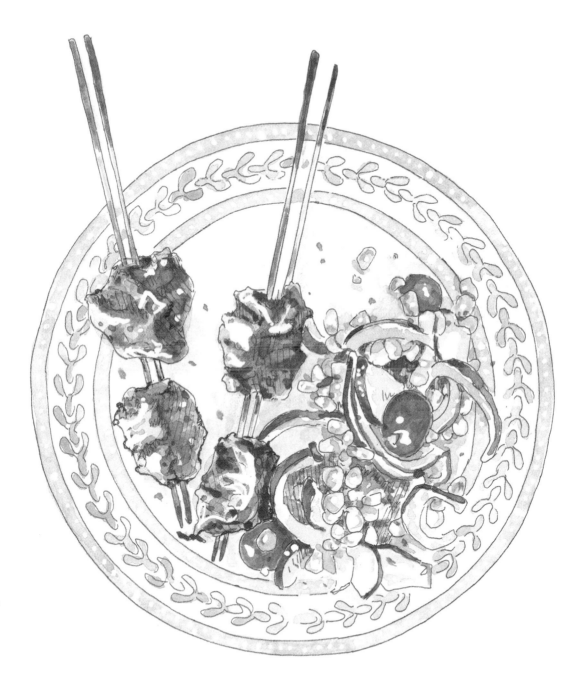

GARLICKY LEMONY GRILLED SHRIMP

Day 1 prep continues! You'll grill delicious shrimp for tomorrow's Garlicky Lemony Grilled Shrimp and Quinoa Bowls and make extra marinade for tonight's Grilled Corn Salad.

¾ cup olive oil

Zest and juice of 1 lemon

¼ cup chopped fresh flat-leaf parsley or other fresh herbs

4 garlic cloves, minced (or 1 teaspoon garlic powder if you're in a hurry)

½ teaspoon table salt

¼ teaspoon ground black pepper

Pinch of cayenne pepper

1 pound peeled and deveined shrimp, medium or large

1. In a jar with a lid, combine the oil, lemon zest and juice, parsley, garlic, salt, pepper, and cayenne and shake to blend. Place the shrimp in a resealable plastic bag and pour one-third of the marinade over the shrimp. (Reserve two-thirds of the marinade for the Grilled Corn Salad.)

2. Marinate the shrimp in the fridge for 30 minutes or up to 2 hours. (If you marinate longer, the acid in the lemons will essentially cook the shrimp.)

3. Preheat the grill to medium, remove the shrimp from the marinade, and place them on skewers. Grill the shrimp for 2 minutes per side, or until they are pink and no longer translucent.

SAVE IT FORWARD—MARINADE: You'll use the remaining marinade tonight for the Grilled Corn Salad (page 127).

SAVE IT FORWARD—SHRIMP: Save the grilled shrimp for tomorrow's Garlicky Lemony Grilled Shrimp and Quinoa Bowls (page 130).

GRILLED CORN SALAD

A terrific companion to eat tonight with the spiedies! A corn salad with fresh corn is one of the delights of summer. But do you know what's not delightful? Shucking corn. I have a trick to share with you, though: if you grill corn in its husk, it's much easier to shuck. The silks are much less sticky!

6 ears corn (a **SAVE-IT-FORWARD** item)

¾ cup red onion slivers (a **SAVE-IT-FORWARD** item)

1 cup medium-diced zucchini

1 cup cherry tomatoes, cut into quarters

6 fresh basil leaves, sliced into strips

Table salt and ground black pepper

Reserved dressing from Garlicky Lemony Grilled Shrimp (page 126), or any bottled Italian dressing

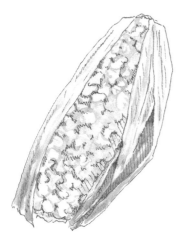

1. Preheat the grill to medium heat.

2. Place each ear of corn, still in the husk and with the silks retained, on the grill and cook for 15 to 20 minutes, occasionally turning until the husks are blackened. Remove from the grill and cool until you can handle, then shuck, de-silk, and cut the corn from the cob.

3. Place two-thirds of the cut corn (from 4 ears) in a large bowl. Add ¼ cup of the onion slivers and the zucchini, tomatoes, basil, and salt and pepper to taste. Right before serving, add just enough of the dressing to coat the veggies lightly, then toss to coat the salad evenly. If you can, save a bit of the dressing for freshening up the leftovers in tomorrow night's meal.

SAVE IT FORWARD—SALAD: Add any leftover salad to the Garlicky Lemony Grilled Shrimp and Quinoa Bowls (page 130) tomorrow, along with any reserved dressing.

SAVE IT FORWARD—CORN: Save the kernels from 2 of the ears of corn for Oklahoma Slaw (page 139) later in the week.

SAVE IT FORWARD—ONION: Reserve ¼ cup of the onion slivers for Watermelon, Feta, and Arugula Salad (page 134) and ¼ cup for Oklahoma Slaw (page 139).

GRILLED PORK TENDERLOIN

2 tablespoons paprika

1 tablespoon garlic powder

2 teaspoons table salt

2 teaspoons ground black pepper

Pork tenderloins, 5 ounces per person (see page 122 for Note on quantities)

2 tablespoons olive oil

Goodness, this grilled pork is good. And easy. Warning: It's going to be hard to resist eating any today, but stay strong— you're prepping it tonight for Days 3 and 5!

1. Preheat the grill to low-medium heat.

2. Combine the dry ingredients in a small bowl. Slather the tenderloins with olive oil and rub the dry ingredients over all the tenderloins. This can be done the night before; place the meat in a resealable plastic bag and refrigerate until you're ready to grill.

3. Grill with the cover closed for 25 to 30 minutes, turning occasionally, until the meat is light pink or an instant-read thermometer registers 145°F.

4. Remove from the grill and let cool a bit before packaging to save for later in the week.

SAVE IT FORWARD—PORK TENDERLOINS: You'll use the grilled pork tenderloins in Cuban Sliders (page 132) and Barbecue Pork Sandwiches (page 137). You'll be making the Cuban Sliders in a couple of days, so it's okay to keep that portion of the pork in the fridge. I would reserve one-third of the pork for Cuban Sliders and two-thirds for Barbecue Pork Sandwiches, but you be the judge! To be cautious, it's best practice to freeze the pork that you're holding for the barbecue meal late in the week. You could even slow-cook the barbecued pork early in the week and freeze it, which would mean you'd only have to reheat it on the day you serve it.

ASIAN FLANK STEAK

Flank steak, 3 to 4 ounces per person (see page 122 for quantity tips)

1½ cups soy sauce (I use low-sodium)

6 garlic cloves, roughly chopped

One 4-inch fresh ginger knob, peeled and sliced into coins

This three-ingredient marinade packs a punch! Again, you must resist eating the steak today so you can take it easy on Day 4.

1. Place all the ingredients in a resealable plastic bag and marinate the steak in the fridge all day or overnight, flipping the bag over periodically if you're around the house. (If you are away from the house, no need to carry a bag of raw meat with you in your purse all day.)

2. Preheat the grill to medium-high.

3. Drain the marinade and toss the flank steak on the grill. Sear the steak undisturbed for 5 minutes, then turn it and sear for another 5 minutes. If you like your meat more well done, no problem: it will cook a bit in the oven when you're reheating it later in the week.

4. Let the steak cool, then wrap it in foil and refrigerate it.

SAVE IT FORWARD—FLANK STEAK: Later in the week, you'll slice the flank steak to go with the quinoa summer rolls (see page 135).

GARLICKY LEMONY GRILLED SHRIMP AND QUINOA BOWLS

¾ cup dry quinoa (a **SAVE-IT-FORWARD** item)

Garlicky Lemony Grilled Shrimp (page 126), saved forward, or boiled shrimp from the seafood counter

Grilled Corn Salad (page 127), saved forward

Bagged coleslaw blend (a **SAVE-IT-FORWARD** item)

Arugula

Fresh flat-leaf parsley, chopped

Sliced radishes or cukes or any other fresh vegetables that you want to throw in!

Reserved dressing from Grilled Corn Salad (page 127) or a bit of drizzled olive oil or bottled Italian or vinaigrette dressing

I have fallen hook, line, and sinker for the bowl trend! I love the simple elements and artistic presentation. I'm a firm believer in beauty! If you're trying to entice kids (or reluctant husbands) into eating something unconventional, a beautiful display can be your secret weapon. There are no precise measurements for each ingredient; you'll just be using what you have on hand to make a bowl that suits each person.

1. To prepare the dry quinoa, read the package directions: some quinoa is prerinsed, and some is not. If yours is not prerinsed, you'll need to rinse it in a mesh strainer for a couple of minutes in cold water, lest your quinoa be bitter. Combine the quinoa and 1½ cups of water in a small saucepan and bring to a boil over medium-high heat. Cover, reduce the heat to low, and simmer until the water is absorbed, 10 to 15 minutes. Most recipes suggest that it will take 20 minutes to cook quinoa, but mine always takes 10 minutes. Quinoa is fully cooked when the seeds burst and reveal the cutest little curlicue tails.

2. Arrange the bowl elements in distinct sections in individual bowls and drizzle the dressing over the top. Use no more than 1 cup of the cooked quinoa among all the bowls. You are the Michelangelo of your kitchen: create your own culinary work of art!

SAVE IT FORWARD—QUINOA: Reserve the rest of the cooked quinoa for quinoa summer rolls (see page 135) later in the week.

SAVE IT FORWARD—CABBAGE SLAW BLEND: Use the slaw blend sparingly in this recipe; save most of it for the quinoa summer rolls (see page 135) and Oklahoma Slaw (page 139).

CUBAN SLIDERS

Cooking spray

24 King's Hawaiian rolls (two 12-packs)

8 tablespoons (1 stick) butter, melted

2 teaspoons Worcestershire sauce

1 tablespoon dried, minced onion (or 1 teaspoon onion powder)

1 tablespoon Dijon mustard

1 tablespoon poppy seeds

24 thin slices deli ham

12 thin slices Swiss cheese (or your favorite cheese)

24 pickle slices (or more if your pickles are small rounds; I use a larger oval)

24 thin slices Grilled Pork Tenderloin (page 128), saved forward

Have you had that classic King's Hawaiian sandwich with the poppy seeds? It's one of my absolute favorites, and I hijacked that recipe and morphed it into another of my favorite sandwiches, the Cuban. This dish is a real crowd-pleaser that can be made ahead a day or so earlier, so keep this recipe in your hip pocket for various occasions. It makes twenty-four slider sandwiches, which is likely too much food for tonight's meal, but if I could be so bold as to boss you around a bit, go ahead and make them all, but divide them into two pans, freezing the second pan before baking. You can pull these babies out of the freezer and bake them from their frozen state—seriously, it will save dinner on some future busy day or make a sweet meal for a new mama. Of course you can just halve the recipe if you like. Serve with Watermelon, Feta, and Arugula Salad (page 134).

1. Preheat the oven to 350°F. Spray two 9 x 13-inch baking pans with cooking spray. Cut each entire slab of rolls through the middle so that you have a top half and a bottom half; you do not want to cut the individual rolls apart at this point.

2. Combine the melted butter, Worcestershire sauce, onion, Dijon, and poppy seeds in a medium bowl. Set aside.

3. Lay the bottom half of each slab of rolls in a greased pan and begin assembling the layers of ingredients. Though you will not break apart the rolls into individual sandwiches until you serve, you will want to layer your ingredients by staying within the outline of each roll. Fold the ham slices so that they are slider-size. Cut the cheese slices in half—you'll use half a cheese slice per roll. Stack the ham, cheese, pickle, and

pork on the bottom layer of rolls, in that order, then add the top layer of rolls.

4. Whisk the melted butter mixture again to combine the ingredients, then spoon evenly over the rolls. Cover with foil, pop the pans into the oven (see Step 5 if you are freezing half the recipe), and bake for 20 to 25 minutes, until the cheese is melted. Uncover and bake for a couple more minutes, until the top rolls get a bit golden.

5. If you took my advice and made extra sliders to freeze, cover the unbaked pan tightly with foil and place in the freezer. Thaw overnight in the fridge before baking, or you can place them in the oven from their frozen state. From frozen, bake at 300°F for an hour. If the sliders are still cool in the middle after an hour, microwave them briefly, then broil for a bit to crisp the tops. I'd caution against putting a glass pan from the freezer into a preheated oven; place the pan in a cold oven and then set the oven temperature so the pan and the oven heat at the same time.

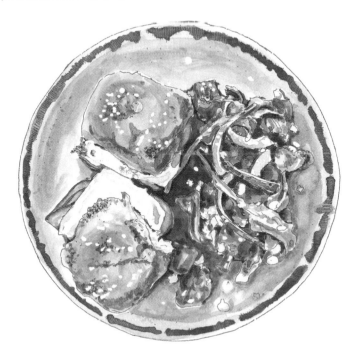

WATERMELON, FETA, AND ARUGULA SALAD

6 cups watermelon chunks

⅓ cup crumbled feta cheese

1 cup arugula

¼ cup red onion slivers (see page 127), saved forward

¼ cup mint leaves, slivered

¼ cup fresh basil leaves, slivered

¼ cup freshly squeezed orange juice (or prepared orange juice)

¼ cup balsamic vinegar

¼ cup olive oil

½ teaspoon table salt, or to taste

You can keep it simple and just serve the Cuban Sliders (page 132) with watermelon slices, but man, oh man, this salad pairs nicely with them.

1. Place the watermelon, feta, arugula, red onion, mint, and basil in a bowl.

2. Combine the orange juice, balsamic vinegar, olive oil, and salt in a jar with a lid and shake until well blended. Drizzle the dressing over the ingredients in the bowl and toss to combine.

ASIAN FLANK STEAK AND QUINOA SUMMER ROLLS with PEANUTTY DIPPING SAUCE

Asian Flank Steak
(page 129), saved forward

QUINOA SUMMER ROLLS

Spring roll rice paper wrappers (see Note on page 136)

Cabbage slaw blend— a scant ⅛ cup per roll (see page 130), saved forward

Cooked quinoa—a scant ⅛ cup per roll (see page 130), saved forward

Red bell pepper strips

Cilantro leaves

DIPPING SAUCE
(MAKE DOUBLE IF YOU'RE BIG DIPPERS!)

½ cup peanut butter

¼ cup plus 2 tablespoons water

3 tablespoons soy sauce (I use low-sodium)

¼ cup white or rice wine vinegar

½ teaspoon crushed red pepper flakes (or more, if you like heat)

You likely have most of the elements of tonight's meal in the fridge already so dinner will be ready in no time. If you have never made summer rolls, they are lots of fun—a real participatory event for the eaters! The quantities for the ingredients will depend on how many rolls you will be making. I envisioned this meal as pictured on page 136, with Asian Flank Steak artfully fanned out on the plate next to a few summer rolls, but my daughter tucked her steak into the summer rolls. You choose!

1. Preheat the oven to 300°F.

2. Place the foil-wrapped flank steak in the oven to warm for 20 to 25 minutes while assembling the summer rolls.

3. To assemble the summer rolls, you will need a bowl of very warm water that is big enough to hold a spring roll wrapper. Submerge one wrapper in the warm water at a time, and let it soak for approximately 15 seconds until it becomes pliable. Remove the wrapper from the water and pat it dry with a clean dish towel. Layer a line of slaw, then quinoa, then bell pepper strips, then cilantro down the middle of the wrapper and follow the rolling instructions on the package of wrappers.

4. To make the dipping sauce, combine the peanut butter, water, soy sauce, vinegar, and red pepper flakes in a medium bowl and whisk vigorously until blended.

5. Remove the steak from the oven and place on a cutting board. Slice the flank steak against the grain into ½-inch-thick slices. Serve alongside the summer rolls and small bowls of the dipping sauce.

TO DO TONIGHT:

Remove the frozen pork tenderloin or already cooked barbecued pork (page 128) from the freezer and let it thaw overnight in the refrigerator.

If you're feeling ambitious, make the Oklahoma Slaw (page 139) tonight, since it gets better after 24 hours!

NOTE ON SPRING ROLL WRAPPERS: These are found in the Asian section of most grocery stores. They look like a tortilla made from rice and become pliable and ready to eat after just a brief soak. They are translucent, so you can see the pretty fillings. I'm not an expert at rolling them, but it's the same method as rolling a burrito. My rolls are a little loose (I'm an amateur!), and I have to use a fork to eat them, but they're still fun. Bonus: rice paper wrappers are low in calories!

BARBECUE PORK SANDWICHES and OKLAHOMA SLAW

Tonight's meal tempts me to write a raft of disclaimers. The barbecued pork is hardly more than barbecue sauce added to your precooked pork. Is that really just too easy to count as a recipe? After all, you've bought my cookbook with your hard-earned money—I don't want to shortchange you!

I quickly reminded myself, though, that because you're using my hocus-pocus meal ideas, you'll actually get a home-cooked meal on the table instead of buying a meal at a restaurant. I don't need to apologize for that, right?! (Thank you for your support as I work through this internal dialogue.)

If you are avoiding bread for one reason or another, serve the barbecue on top of a baked potato or the slaw—delicious!

1 yellow onion, thinly sliced

Grilled Pork Tenderloin (page 128), saved forward

1 (12-ounce) bottle of your favorite barbecue sauce (we like Head Country, made in Oklahoma!)

Buns (or baked potatoes, if you have more time)

Oklahoma Slaw (page 139)

1. Place the onion in the crock of a slow cooker and add an inch of water to the crock. Place the cooked tenderloin on top and cook for at least 4 hours on low, though you can cook it all day. Remove the meat and chop it. Discard the onion, then return the pork to the slow cooker and add enough barbecue sauce to coat it well. Cook on high until the meat absorbs the flavor, about 15 minutes.

2. Serve on buns (buttered and grilled is wonderfully over the top), with the Oklahoma Slaw either on the side or tucked into the sandwich. If you're serving with baked potatoes, cut the potatoes lengthwise and top them with the barbecued pork.

OKLAHOMA SLAW

We Oklahomans love ranch dressing, so of course we think it makes a suitable substitution for the mayonnaise in traditional coleslaw.

8 ounces bagged coleslaw blend (see page 130), saved forward

Kernels from 2 ears corn (see page 127), saved forward, or ¾ cup canned Mexicorn

¼ cup red onion slivers (see page 127), saved forward, diced

½ jalapeño, seeded and finely chopped

½ cup ranch dressing

¼ teaspoon white vinegar

¼ teaspoon ground cumin

¼ teaspoon garlic powder

Table salt and ground black pepper

Combine the coleslaw blend, corn, red onion, and jalapeño in a large bowl. In a separate small bowl, whisk the ranch dressing with the vinegar, cumin, garlic powder, and salt and pepper to taste. Pour this mixture over the vegetables and toss to combine. If you have time to prepare and refrigerate the slaw a bit ahead, the flavors will meld nicely, or just serve immediately if you're in a time crunch.

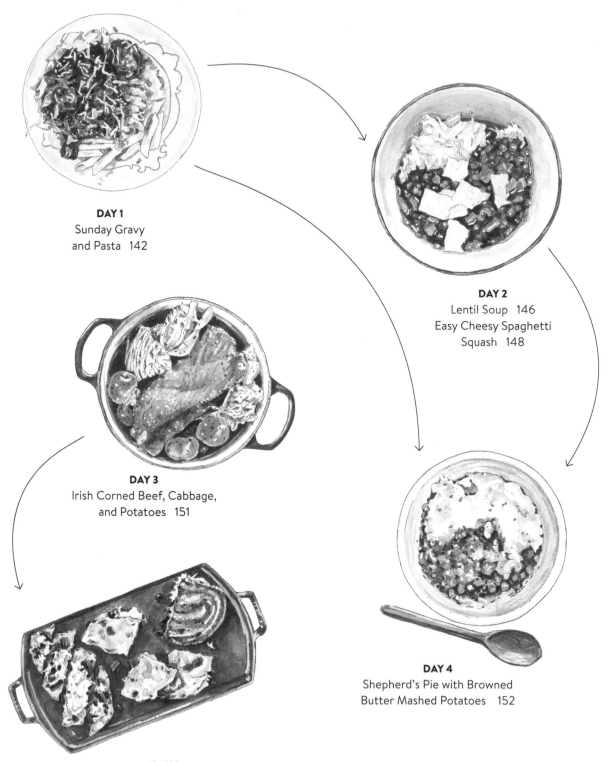

DAY 1
Sunday Gravy
and Pasta   142

DAY 2
Lentil Soup   146
Easy Cheesy Spaghetti
Squash   148

DAY 3
Irish Corned Beef, Cabbage,
and Potatoes   151

DAY 4
Shepherd's Pie with Browned
Butter Mashed Potatoes   152

DAY 5
Reubens Your Way   155

Comfort Foods from Across the Pond Week

We're crossing the Atlantic Ocean this week to cook England's, Ireland's, and Italy's classic family comfort foods. The Sunday gravy takes a bit of time, but besides being just plain delicious, it allows you to reimagine the components in a couple of other meals. Shepherd's Pie can be time-consuming, but I'm sharing all my shortcuts with you to make it a doable weekday meal.

SUNDAY GRAVY AND PASTA

BRACIOLE, A SAVE-IT-FORWARD ITEM

4 pieces (1½ total pounds) round steak (or flank, skirt, or sirloin steak)

1 egg, whisked

½ cup grated Parmesan cheese

½ cup bread crumbs (I use canned gluten-free bread crumbs)

½ cup chopped fresh flat-leaf parsley

SUNDAY GRAVY, A SAVE-IT-FORWARD ITEM

3 pounds beef short ribs, a **SAVE-IT-FORWARD** item

Olive oil, as needed

4 links sweet Italian sausage (a **SAVE-IT-FORWARD** item)

½ cup red wine (optional, for flavor), or chicken or beef broth or water

2 garlic cloves, minced, plus 5 whole cloves

Two 6-ounce cans tomato paste

Two 8-ounce cans tomato sauce

Two 15-ounce cans crushed tomatoes

1 yellow onion

1 carrot, peeled

6 fresh basil leaves, cut into strips

When you live on the Oklahoma prairie, the opportunities for authentic Italian food are virtually nil. While traveling, I stumbled upon Sunday gravy and was utterly smitten, and I have been sidling up to any Italian I can find to learn its mysterious ways ever since. Italian cooks don't write these recipes down; the next generation absorbs them from Nonna at the stove.

The gravy in this recipe is not a "gravy" in the Oklahoma definition of gravy. Since it's not brown or cream, we Okies would call this "marinara," but I'm sure Italians would balk at that. Even among Italian Americans, there's a raging battle about whether to dub this "sauce" or "gravy." Some Italian Facebook groups even threaten expulsion if anyone picks a fight over what to call it. Whatever you call it, it's good. And it's the kind of meal that memories are made of, which is why those sentimental Italians have made it part of their family culture.

To sum it up, Sunday gravy is a simple tomato-based sauce simmered for a few hours with a variety of meats—the greater the variety of meats, the better. As far as I can tell, most Italians seem to make Sunday gravy with pork or lamb neck bones, but I couldn't find them in Oklahoma—it's beef country in these parts! Here I use beef short ribs (the bones impart flavor) and Italian sausage, and I'll be making braciole (stuffed, rolled, and tied round steak) to add to the assortment. We'll be using the leftover short ribs and braciole in Shepherd's Pie (page 152), but if you want to simplify things and are skipping that meal, you could substitute premade meatballs from the freezer section for the braciole in this recipe.

½ to 1 teaspoon crushed red pepper flakes

1½ teaspoons table salt, or to taste

½ teaspoon ground black pepper

Cooked sturdy pasta of your choice (such as rigatoni), for serving

Grated Parmesan, for serving

Special tool: cooking twine

1. To prepare the braciole, place each piece of steak between sheets of plastic wrap, or on a silicone baking mat, if you have one, that's folded over the meat. The plastic wrap or silicone mat will keep little pieces of meat from flying all over your kitchen. Pound each steak ¼ or ½ inch thick. (My pounding arm tuckered out at ½ inch, and that thickness worked fine!)

2. In a small bowl, combine the egg, Parmesan, bread crumbs, and parsley.

3. Slather the Parmesan mixture on one side of each piece of meat. Roll each steak like a jelly roll, starting from the shortest side, then secure the roll with cooking twine at the ends and in the middle. Set aside.

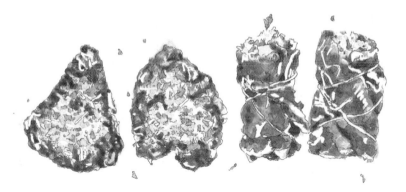

4. To make the Sunday gravy, in a large (at least 5 quart) heavy-bottomed pot with a lid, brown the short ribs for 2 to 3 minutes on each side. (Since short ribs contain a lot of fat, there's no need to add oil to the pot.) Remove the short ribs to a large plate. Add the braciole to the pot and brown for 2 to 3 minutes per side. (There should be enough fat left in the pot from the short ribs to brown the braciole, but if not, add a bit of olive oil.) Remove the braciole to the plate with

the short ribs. Next, sear the sausage until browned on two sides, adding a bit more oil to the pot to keep it from sticking if necessary. Remove to the plate as well.

5. Deglaze the pot over medium-high heat with the wine (or broth or water), scraping up all the delicious little bits. This is a very hot, sizzling process, so take care—don't have your face over the pot! Add the minced garlic and tomato paste and cook on medium-low until the garlic is fragrant, about 1 minute, stirring often. Add the tomato sauce, crushed tomatoes, onion, carrot, garlic cloves, basil, red pepper flakes, salt, and black pepper. Return the browned meats to the pot. (If you're using prepared frozen meatballs instead of braciole, add them now—no need to thaw!)

6. Stir to combine, cover the pot, and simmer for 3 to 4 hours over low heat, occasionally stirring to prevent sticking. The meat will be fully cooked early in the process, but the long, slow simmer helps the flavors meld.

7. To serve, place the meat on a platter, cutting the sausage and braciole into smaller pieces if desired and covering with foil to keep warm while you tend to the sauce. Discard the garlic cloves, onion, carrot, and kitchen twine and skim the visible fat from the surface of the sauce. If you have an immersion blender, you can give the sauce a quick whiz right in the pot, but that's optional. Ladle the sauce over pasta, nestle the meat alongside, and sprinkle Parmesan on the top.

SAVE IT FORWARD—SUNDAY GRAVY: Reserve ½ cup of the gravy for Lentil Soup (page 146) and 2 tablespoons for Shepherd's Pie (page 152).

SAVE IT FORWARD—SAUSAGE: If you have any leftover sausage, slice it and add it to the Lentil Soup (page 146).

SAVE IT FORWARD—SHORT RIBS AND BRACIOLE: These are your most important leftovers. You'll want to save 3 to 4 cups of meat if possible (although I have a trick to augment the meat later if needed). Chop the meat into bite-size pieces while still warm, removing the fat as you go. The filling in the braciole will add flavor to the Shepherd's Pie (page 152), so don't discard it! You can store both kinds of meat together in the fridge.

LENTIL SOUP

Lentil soup . . . ahh, does it get more elemental and comforting than a steaming bowl of lentil-y goodness? To make it a more substantial meal, pair it with a side of Easy Cheesy Spaghetti Squash (page 148). I put the squash right in the bowl with my soup, and it's delicious! My guys are skeptical about lentils, so I always serve this soup with crusty bread to sop up the thick, flavorful broth. I'm not proud of this, but my boys' favorite bread is the garlic Texas toast from the freezer aisle, browned on our cast-iron griddle (the oven works, too, obviously). I skip the bread so I can have a second bowl of soup!

1½ cups brown lentils

1 tablespoon olive oil

1 cup medium-diced peeled carrots

1 cup medium-diced celery

1 cup medium-diced yellow onion

8 cups (2 quarts) Overnight Chicken Broth (page 268) or other chicken broth

½ cup Sunday Gravy (page 142), saved forward, or see Note

Cooked sliced Italian sausage (see page 144), saved forward (optional)

Table salt and ground black pepper

1. Rinse the lentils and remove any funky-looking ones.

2. In a large soup pot over medium-low heat, heat the olive oil. Add the carrots, celery, and onion and sauté until a bit tender, 4 to 5 minutes. Add the chicken broth, lentils, Sunday Gravy, sausage, and salt and pepper to taste. Bring to a boil, turn down to a simmer, and cook for around 15 minutes, or until the lentils are tender. That's it! So simple.

NOTE ON SUBSTITUTION: If you didn't make Sunday Gravy earlier in the week, you can substitute 1 tablespoon tomato paste and 1 teaspoon Italian seasoning.

SAVE IT FORWARD—LENTILS: The lentils from your leftover soup can add some bulk to Shepherd's Pie (page 152). The recipe calls for 4 cups of meat, and if you run short, supplement with lentils extracted from the soup. So, save the soup in case you need some emergency lentils—and if not, you'll have the leftovers for lunch this week!

EASY CHEESY SPAGHETTI SQUASH

1 spaghetti squash

2 wedges Laughing Cow cheese (see Note on page 149)

Pinch of cayenne pepper

¼ teaspoon garlic powder

Table salt and ground black pepper

You can make this as a cheesy side dish, but the cooked spaghetti squash is absolutely delicious as the bottom layer in your bowl of Lentil Soup (page 146). Just spoon the soup over the strands to add a little more texture, nutrition, and flavor. I add quite a bit to my bowl because I love the taste, but my teenagers balk when I try this move in their bowls. Sheesh . . . no imagination!

I generally roast my spaghetti squash in the oven when I have forty-five minutes or so; a slow cooker works well if you have half a day. I use the microwave for this dish because it takes about the same amount of time as the lentil soup.

1. Prick the outside of the spaghetti squash ten times. Place it in the microwave and cook on high for 5 to 6 minutes, depending on the size. Turn it over and cook for another 5 to 6 minutes, until the skin gives when you touch it. Let it cool for at least 5 minutes, until you can handle it. Cut it in half lengthwise and remove the seeds. Use a fork to separate all the squash strands and place them in a bowl. If the squash is not separating into strands, cook it a bit longer. Reserve whichever squash half is more intact.

2. Add the cheese, cayenne, garlic powder, and salt and pepper to taste to the bowl of squash and stir until melted. If necessary, microwave again briefly to assist with the melting process. Return the squash mixture to its shell for serving (unless you are taking my advice and spooning it directly into your lentil soup bowl!).

NOTE: If you haven't discovered Laughing Cow cheese, it's a wonder! Low in calories and super-melty (particularly the light variety), it packs a cheesy punch. I like it schmeared on crackers, so I generally have it in the fridge, but you can sub cream cheese and a little grated cheese.

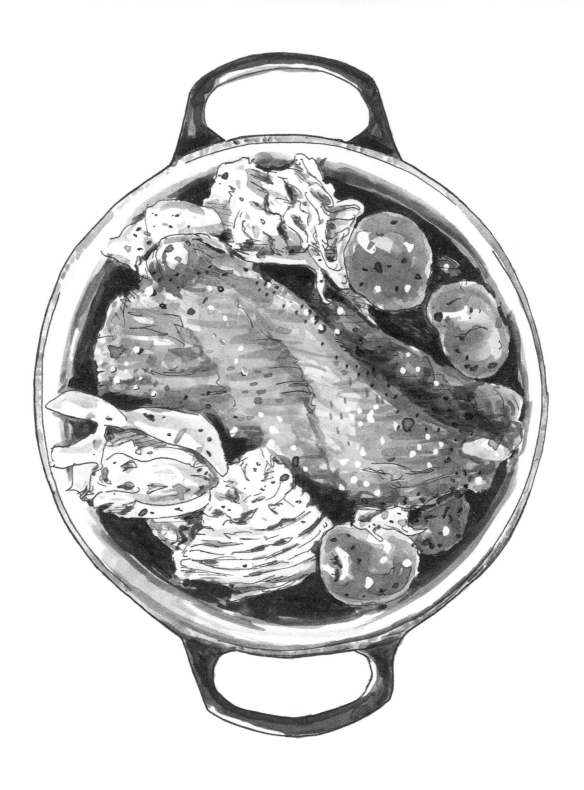

IRISH CORNED BEEF, CABBAGE, AND POTATOES

8 to 12 baby red or Yukon Gold potatoes

One 4-pound package corned beef brisket with a spice packet (a **SAVE-IT-FORWARD** item)

4 cups (1 quart) Overnight Chicken Broth (page 268) or other chicken or beef broth

2 bay leaves

½ head green cabbage, cut into wedges or chopped, per your preference

Throw these ingredients into the slow cooker in five minutes flat in the morning and run out the door and you will come home from work to a legit meal. There's just one caveat: the cabbage will take much less time to cook than the corned beef and potatoes, so you'll have to add that thirty minutes before dinnertime. Save the date for March 17: this makes a fun St. Patrick's Day dinner!

1. Place the potatoes in the crock of a slow cooker. Sprinkle half the corned beef seasoning packet over the potatoes. Place the corned beef brisket over the potatoes, fat side up, then sprinkle the rest of the seasoning on the beef. Pour the broth into the crock and add the bay leaves.

2. Set the slow cooker to low and cook for 8 to 9 hours or so, until the meat is fork tender. If you're getting a late start, cook on high for part of that time. Remove the brisket and potatoes from the crock and cover with foil to keep warm. Discard the bay leaf. Add the cabbage to the crock, set it to high, and cook for 30 minutes, or to your liking.

3. Slice the meat across the grain (reserving a large uncut piece; see Save It Forward—Corned Beef below) and serve it with the potatoes and cabbage. My kids like to make their own mashed potatoes on their plates with an unholy amount of butter. I think the broth makes the potatoes plenty flavorful.

SAVE IT FORWARD—CORNED BEEF: You'll use 2 to 3 ounces of reserved meat per person for Reubens Your Way (page 155), so wrap the meat up whole and slice it just before using.

SHEPHERD'S PIE with BROWNED BUTTER MASHED POTATOES

This is my boys' all-time favorite meal, the one they ask for on their birthdays. If you make it entirely from scratch, it can be a bit time-consuming, but I've taken some shortcuts without shortchanging the flavor. I shamelessly use a packet of brown gravy mix. There. I said it: packaged gravy mix. I promise there are enough homemade components here that the flavor won't have that telltale packaged taste—trust me. Another shortcut is using an Instant Pot. If you don't have one, just boil the potatoes on the stove until tender.

The over-the-top element of this dish is the browned butter in the mashed potatoes. It's so quick and easy—please don't skip this step!

MASHED POTATOES

2½ pounds small Yukon Gold potatoes, unpeeled

8 tablespoons (1 stick) butter

⅓ cup milk

½ teaspoon Lawry's Seasoned Salt, or your favorite blend

½ teaspoon table salt

½ teaspoon ground black pepper

1 package McCormick Brown Gravy Mix (or your favorite brand)

1 teaspoon Worcestershire sauce

2 tablespoons sauce from Sunday Gravy (page 142), saved forward, or 1 tablespoon tomato paste

4 cups combined cooked meat from Sunday Gravy (page 142) and cooked lentils from Lentil Soup (page 146), saved forward (see Note on page 154)

One 10-ounce package frozen mixed vegetables (or frozen peas and carrots), unthawed

Buttered bread, for serving (optional)

1. Preheat the oven to 350°F.

2. To make the mashed potatoes, add the potatoes and water to cover to an Instant Pot. Set the timer for 12 minutes on high pressure. When the cycle ends, do a quick release of pressure, then drain the water, leaving the potatoes in the pot. Turn the Instant Pot to the sauté setting for just a couple of minutes to evaporate any remaining water.

3. Meanwhile, melt the butter in a small pan or skillet. As the butter cooks, the butter solids will fall to the bottom of the pan; stir frequently to keep them from burning. (It is easier to monitor the color of the butter if you use a stainless-steel pan or one with a light-colored interior.) Remove the butter from the heat when it is fragrant and the color of iced tea.

4. Mash the potatoes in the pot with a potato masher (or a ricer, if you're a kitchen gadget person); it's a handy shortcut to mash with the peels on, but you might want to remove big pieces of peel. And don't overmash or your potatoes will be gummy. Add the browned butter (including the solids at the bottom), the milk, and the seasoned salt, table salt, and pepper and stir to incorporate.

5. To make the meat mixture, prepare the brown gravy in a small saucepan according to the package directions, cooking until the gravy is thick. Add the Worcestershire sauce and Sunday Gravy and stir to combine.

6. In a 9 x 9-inch baking pan, stir together the gravy, meat, lentils, and frozen vegetables. Your mixture will be the consistency of a thick stew. If it is too thick, you can thin it with a bit of broth from the soup.

7. Top the meat mixture with a layer of mashed potatoes. You may or may not have enough potatoes to cover the meat completely; it's okay to have some open spaces.

8. Bake for 40 to 45 minutes, until the filling is bubbly and the potatoes are lightly browned. Scoop and serve. This is a one-bowl sort of meal, though my guys usually add some buttered bread on the side.

NOTE ON LENTILS: You'll likely not have 4 cups of meat left over from the Sunday Gravy (page 142), so you'll augment it with the lentils from the leftover Lentil Soup (page 146). Scoop out the lentils from the soup with a slotted spoon and let them drain well in a mesh strainer—the drier the lentils, the better. Add the lentils to the reserved meat to make 4 cups of meat and lentils.

TIME-SAVING TIP: Use the same pan to make the browned butter and the gravy. Just give the pan a quick wipe in between.

REUBENS YOUR WAY

The best part about making corned beef is having the leftovers to make Reubens! Since I live in Small Town on the Prairie, there's no rye bread to be found for many miles. So, I generally make these as quesadillas with flour tortillas or flatbread, which is also lovely grilled. The amounts for the Reubens are just general: pile on each ingredient according to your preference. My family skips the sauerkraut—they're clearly addled in the head.

Rye bread, flatbread, or tortillas

Thousand Island dressing

Swiss or provolone cheese, sliced thin

Corned beef (see page 151), saved forward, sliced as thinly as possible

Drained sauerkraut (canned or refrigerated—both are great!)

Butter

1. Assemble the sandwich/quesadilla. I like to have a thin schmear of Thousand Island on the top and bottom, a thin slice of cheese on the top and bottom, and a layer of corned beef and sauerkraut nestled in the middle.

2. Heat a large nonstick pan or griddle over medium-low heat and melt some butter in the areas on which you will place the sandwiches. Place the sandwiches in the pan and cook on both sides until the cheese melts and the bread or tortilla is toasty and browned. Cut into halves and serve.

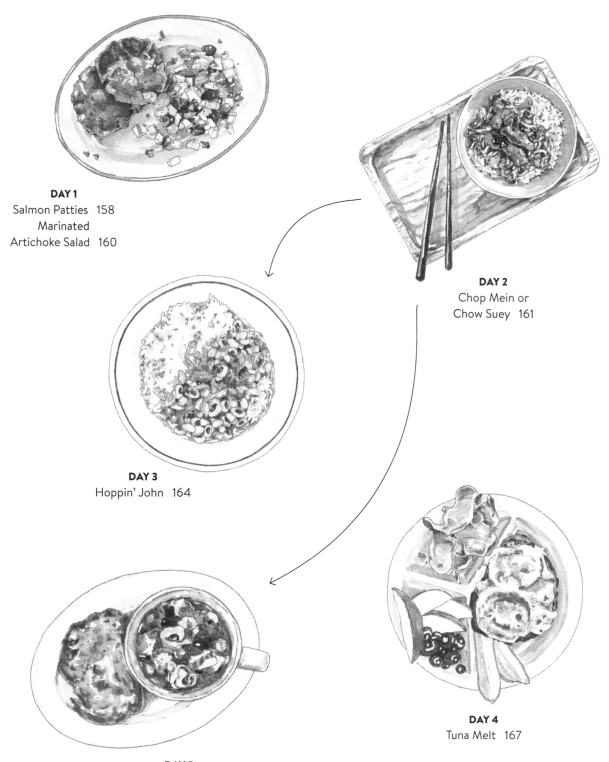

DAY 1
Salmon Patties 158
Marinated
Artichoke Salad 160

DAY 2
Chop Mein or
Chow Suey 161

DAY 3
Hoppin' John 164

DAY 4
Tuna Melt 167

DAY 5
Pantry Minestrone 168

Pantry Item Week

The coronavirus pandemic caught us all by surprise, didn't it? I have a few abiding lessons (scars?) that will stay with me. For one, I don't think I'll ever have a bare pantry again. I haven't become a prepper by any means, but I think it's wise to have some canned goods on hand so one can always get a meal on the table. In that vein, this week's meals primarily consist of pantry items, with a few fresh or frozen things thrown in. In a disaster, though, you could skip the fresh vegetables and still make the meal from just the pantry items and a little bit of pork from the freezer.

Okay, enough doom—let me pitch this week's meals another way: if you have just a few pantry items on hand, you'll have the makings of a quick meal without adding a trip to the store!

SALMON PATTIES

1 small zucchini, trimmed and unpeeled

1 teaspoon table salt

1 egg

2 tablespoons plain yogurt or sour cream

½ cup flour (I use gluten-free)

½ cup cornmeal

2 teaspoons baking powder

½ teaspoon Old Bay seasoning (or your favorite seasoning blend)

¼ teaspoon ground black pepper

1 teaspoon minced garlic

¼ cup grated or finely chopped yellow onion

One 14.75-ounce can salmon, drained

2 tablespoons olive oil

1 tablespoon butter

Basil Aioli (page 222), mayonnaise, or sour cream, for serving

I didn't grow up eating salmon patties, but I've become a believer. As a Catholic, I opt for meatless meals on Fridays, but when you live in a small town on the prairie, you have zero options for fresh fish (well, except for maybe fishing in a ranch pond, but this is Pantry Week!). Canned salmon to the rescue! When doctored up, then lightly fried, the patties make a delightful meal, particularly when paired with the flavorful Marinated Artichoke Salad (page 160).

1. Grate the zucchini on the fine side of a box grater, sprinkle it lightly with ½ teaspoon of the salt, and spread it out on a couple of paper towels to let it release its moisture while you're prepping the other ingredients.

2. In a medium bowl, lightly mix together the egg and yogurt, then stir in the flour, cornmeal, baking powder, Old Bay, pepper, and the remaining ½ teaspoon salt. Remove all the moisture you can from the zucchini by pressing another paper towel on top of it, squeezing and squishing. Add the zucchini, garlic, onion, and salmon to the flour mixture and mix gently but thoroughly.

3. Form the mixture into 6 to 7 patties (or make them smaller if you prefer). Don't over-press them or they will be too dense.

4. Heat a large skillet over medium heat, then add the oil and butter and heat until a few drops of water sizzle when flicked into the skillet. Cook the patties for 2 to 3 minutes on each side, until very golden brown.

5. Serve with Basil Aioli, mayonnaise, or sour cream.

LUNCH BITS AND BOBS: *My daughter, Meg, made what she considers to be a revolutionary discovery. She and I were testing recipes, and she made a salmon taco from a leftover salmon patty. She broke a patty into pieces and put it inside a warm tortilla schmeared with Hummus (page 209), then added some leftover roasted veggies. Her mama was delighted by both the taste and her ingenuity.*

MARINATED ARTICHOKE SALAD

One 6-ounce jar marinated artichoke hearts, undrained

½ cup salad olives (olives with pimientos), juice reserved

1 handful spinach

1 handful arugula

1 cup cherry tomatoes (or whatever you have!)

1 small or medium yellow or zucchini squash

1 small cucumber

¼ to ½ cup crumbled feta cheese

Table salt and ground black pepper

Disclaimer: This isn't strictly a pantry dish because, hey, it's a salad, man. I'm including it in Pantry Week for two reasons: (1) It's an absolute gem, beloved by all who eat it and (2) it starts with two humble pantry items: marinated artichoke hearts and salad olives. You won't even need to add dressing, because the artichokes and olives combine with the tomatoes' juice to make a dressing.

Though this may seem like a large quantity, I'm hoping you'll have some left over for lunch salads; it keeps surprisingly well. Add a protein and it's a complete meal for **Lunch Bits and Bobs**.

1. Chop all the veggies, combine them in a salad bowl, and sprinkle on the feta and salt and pepper to taste. If you happen to have one of those circular-bladed knives that rock back and forth (a mezzaluna, for you fancy word people!), this is an excellent time to use it. I cut the cherry tomatoes in half and cut the squash and cucumber in chunks. Then I become a ninja warrior with my fancy mezzaluna. If you don't have one, just chop each ingredient into reasonably small pieces.

2. If you're lucky enough to have leftovers, and if the salad dries out a bit, just add a bit of olive juice, or water to moisten it.

CHOP MEIN OR CHOW SUEY

1½ pounds pork loin chops, cut into ½-inch strips

¼ cup plus 2 tablespoons soy sauce

¾ cup Overnight Chicken Broth (page 268) or other chicken broth, or ¾ cup water plus 1 teaspoon chicken base

1 tablespoon molasses (or 1 teaspoon brown sugar)

2 tablespoons cornstarch or arrowroot powder

¼ teaspoon ground black pepper

2 tablespoons sesame oil (or vegetable oil)

1 cup slivered yellow onion

1 cup ¼-inch-diced celery

2 cups sliced mushrooms

Two 14-ounce cans chop suey vegetables, drained

Cooked rice, for serving (a **SAVE-IT-FORWARD** item; see page 162)

I know, I know . . . it's Chow Mein and Chop Suey, but my convoluted title is indicative of my state of knowledge about what this recipe is or should be. Chow mein was the dinner I pleaded with my mom to make from the red-checkered Betty Crocker cookbook. My seven-year-old self loved this meal! I had long since forgotten about it until I started scrabbling around in the pantry when we hunkered down during the pandemic. Lo and behold, I found a can of chop suey vegetables, which I remembered was the base ingredient. Though I recalled that my childhood recipe included chow mein noodles, I ditched them since I didn't want to waste my precious carbs on something not that flavorful. I think my version, then, more resembles chop suey. This is far from traditional Chinese food, but I know what I like, and so here's my hybrid version of the two dishes.

Though the recipe includes fresh vegetables and pork, the signature ingredient is that can of chop suey veggies. But you can sub in an equal amount of canned water chestnuts, bamboo shoots, and baby corn. If you're trying to stock your kitchen for a disaster (or just the chaos of everyday life!), it's great to have pork loin chops in the freezer because they're quick-cooking and versatile.

Be sure to have all the ingredients prepped and ready, as this comes together very quickly!

1. In a medium bowl, toss the strips of pork in the 2 tablespoons of soy sauce and let the pork marinate. Set aside.

2. Make the sauce: In a medium bowl, whisk the broth, the remaining ¼ cup soy sauce, the molasses, cornstarch, and pepper.

3. Heat a large, deep skillet over medium heat. Add the oil and heat until a drop of water sizzles in the pan. Add the pork to the pan and sauté until it has lost most of its pink color, about 3 minutes. Add the onion, celery, and mushrooms and sauté until the vegetables are slightly tender, about 3 minutes. Add the chop suey vegetables and sauté for 2 minutes, until heated throughout.

4. Add the sauce to the pan, stir, and cook for 3 to 4 minutes, or until thickened and bubbly. Serve over rice.

SAVE IT FORWARD—RICE: Double the amount of rice you would typically cook so you can save some forward for Hoppin' John (page 164) and Pantry Minestrone (page 168).

HOPPIN' JOHN

Three 16-ounce cans
black-eyed peas,
undrained

One 10-ounce can diced
tomatoes and green
chiles, mild or original

2 cups Overnight Chicken
Broth (page 268) or other
chicken broth

1 ham hock (or 1 cup diced
ham)

1 teaspoon minced garlic

1 medium yellow onion,
roughly chopped

1 bay leaf

Table salt and ground
black pepper

Cooked rice (see page
162), saved forward, for
serving

This is my Oklahoma take on the classic Southern black-eyed-pea dish. Oklahomans are not quite Southern, so we rarely eat this dish except to satisfy the New Year's Day tradition. Disclaimer: My husband, John, typically detests black-eyed peas, but he thought this was "pretty good!" (with a tone of surprise in his voice). Serving this dish over rice and keeping it brothy makes it more soup-like, if that helps placate any of the black-eyed-pea haters in your family. Me? I could eat Hoppin' John every week!

Most of the items in this dish are from the pantry, except for the onion and the ham hock. If you've avoided ham hocks because they're freakish looking, I get it. I urge you, though, to try them just one time. They often come in packages of two or three, so I tightly wrap the remaining hocks in plastic wrap and pop them in a freezer bag and then into the freezer. If you ever want to give a soup a meaty flavor but there's no meat in the fridge, just pull a ham hock out of the freezer and throw it in the soup pot while still frozen. So handy!

Sautéed Spinach (page 13) makes a great side dish for beans or peas. I would probably skip the heavy cream for this pairing and just cook plain ol' greens.

1. You can cook this dish in a slow cooker for 6 to 8 hours on low or 4 to 6 hours on high. Just throw everything in the crock and walk away. It's also the perfect dish for an Instant Pot—set it for just 12 minutes on manual pressure with a quick release. For stovetop cooking, combine the peas, tomatoes and chiles, broth, ham hock, garlic, onion, and bay leaf in a soup pot, stir, bring to a boil, cover, and cook over medium-low heat for 30 minutes so the flavors meld.

2. Remove the ham hock. Pick off any ham from the hock and add it back into the beans. Discard the bay leaf. Season with salt and pepper to taste.

3. To serve, reheat the rice in the microwave: sprinkle some water over it to moisten it a bit, cover the dish, and microwave until warm. Spoon the rice into a bowl and ladle the Hoppin' John on top. Happy New Year! Or happy Tuesday!

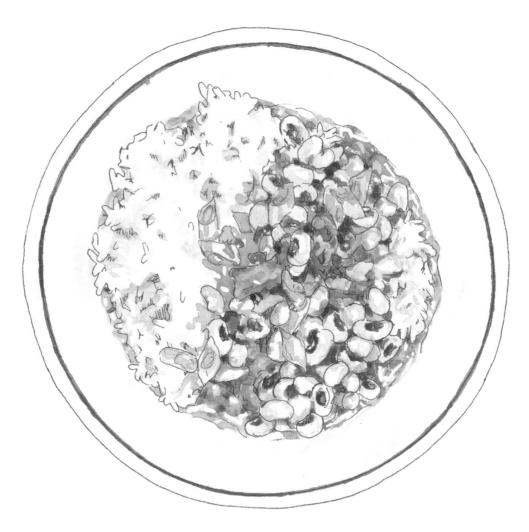

TUNA MELT

Tuna is one of those ever-ready pantry staples that can help you get a meal on the table in no time. Paired with marinated artichokes and capers, wow—this isn't your mother's tuna melt (not that there's anything wrong with your mama's tuna)! Skip the tomatoes for a purely pantry meal. Serve with pickles, chips, fruit—keep it simple!

6 slices sturdy bread, such as Italian

10 ounces tuna, cans or pouches

One 7.5-ounce jar (½ cup) marinated artichoke hearts, roughly chopped, 1 tablespoon of the marinade reserved

¼ cup finely chopped yellow onion

2 tablespoons capers, drained

1 teaspoon Worcestershire sauce

3 tablespoons mayonnaise

Table salt and ground black pepper

3 or 4 Roma tomatoes (or, even better, an equivalent of homegrown tomatoes!)

6 slices Swiss cheese, or cheese of your choice

1. Preheat the oven to 375°F.

2. Spread out the bread slices on a sheet pan and toast in the oven for 2 to 3 minutes per side, until nicely toasted (keep your eye on them so they don't burn!).

3. Meanwhile, in a large bowl, combine the tuna, artichoke hearts and marinade, onion, capers, Worcestershire sauce, and mayonnaise and toss to combine. Taste the mixture and add salt and pepper as desired.

4. Leaving the toast on the sheet pan, spread each piece with tuna mixture. Top each with a layer of sliced tomatoes, then a slice of cheese. Bake for 10 minutes, until the cheese is melted. Turn on the broiler and broil briefly until the cheese is golden brown.

PANTRY MINESTRONE

One 15-ounce can Great Northern beans, drained

One 15-ounce can kidney beans, drained

One 15-ounce can chickpeas, drained

One 14.5-ounce can diced tomatoes

2 cups chopped veggies, fresh or frozen (optional, see Note)

6 cups (1½ quarts) Overnight Chicken Broth (page 268) or other chicken broth

1 cup cooked rice (see page 162), saved forward

1 tablespoon tomato paste (optional)

3 tablespoons prepared basil pesto

1 tablespoon Worcestershire sauce

2 teaspoons minced garlic

⅛ to ¼ teaspoon crushed red pepper flakes, depending on your heat tolerance

Table salt and ground black pepper

1 cup pasta, such as a short penne, including gluten-free

Did you know there's such a thing as jarred basil pesto, usually found near the dry pasta in the grocery store? It's pretty darned good, and it's handy to have in the pantry. You won't need much for this soup, so you can use the leftovers on pasta, as a pizza sauce, and as a component in weeks 11 and 12. The basil pesto gives this minestrone its signature flavor. If you have a tube of tomato paste in your pantry or fridge, it's the perfect time to use it since you only need 1 tablespoon. (Skip it if you don't!) Serve with crusty bread and a vinaigrette-y salad.

1. This is a perfect recipe for an Instant Pot, if you have one. Just dump all the ingredients in and set it for 5 minutes on manual pressure, with a quick release. (If you're subbing a smaller or larger pasta, it may affect the time.)

2. To cook on the stovetop, in a large pot or Dutch oven combine the beans, tomatoes, veggies, broth, rice, tomato paste, pesto, Worcestershire, garlic, red pepper flakes, and salt and pepper to taste. Bring to a boil, then reduce the heat to a simmer and cook, uncovered, for 15 minutes. Add the pasta and simmer until the pasta is tender (see the package instructions for approximate timing).

NOTE: I almost didn't include veggies because I was trying to make this a strictly pantry meal. It's a simple, serviceable soup without the veggies, but veggies take the soup to the next level. Use whatever you have on hand: carrots, celery, zucchini, green beans, mushrooms—clean out your produce drawer. Frozen veggies work, too.

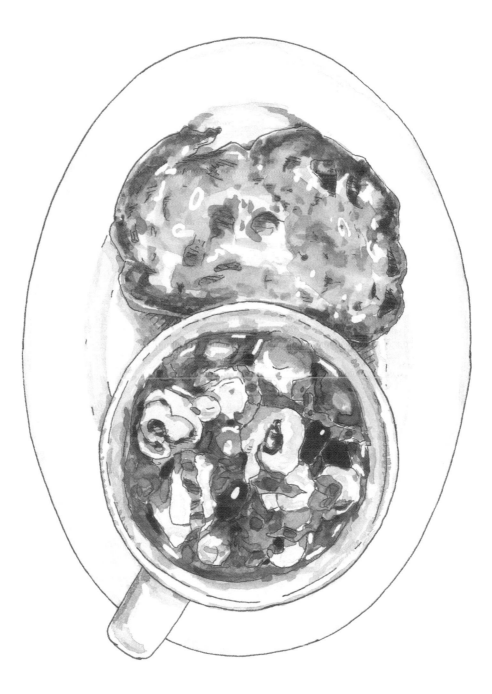

DAY 1
Italian Beef Tips over Rice
173

DAY 2
Stromboli 174

DAY 3
Mexican Beef Stew 176

DAY 4
Creamy Chicken and
Wild Rice Soup 177
Toasty Pinwheels 179

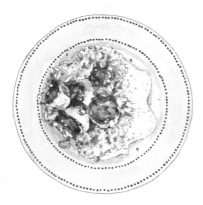

DAY 5
Seared Scallops with Basil Pesto
Cream Sauce and Orzo 180

WEEK 11
Shortcut Week

Sometimes a gal (or guy!) just needs to cut a few culinary corners. This week we'll be using a packaged ingredient or two, and we'll make good use of a store-bought rotisserie chicken—or make Everyday Slow Cooker Chicken (page 266). Scallops are their own shortcut for a restaurant-worthy meal in a flash!

ADVANCE PREP

Rotisserie Chicken

We're making use of a trusty deli-cooked rotisserie chicken this week. To streamline your week, you may want to debone it and cut it into bite-size pieces at the start of the week. The average chicken will yield 4 cups of meat, and you'll use 1 cup in the Stromboli (page 174) and 2 cups in the Creamy Chicken and Wild Rice Soup (page 177). You'll have 1 remaining cup of cooked chicken. What to do with it?

- Add it to a green salad for a healthy lunch!
- Make chicken salad (see page 44).
- Freeze it with 2 cups of broth so it will be ready for a quick chicken soup when you have an ailing loved one.
- Combine the chicken with cooked pasta, a bit of chicken broth (or chicken base and water), and some jarred Alfredo sauce (left over from this week). You can eat it right out of the pot or bake it with some shredded cheese on top. A tip from my youngest son: add a bit of marinara from this week's Toasty Pinwheels.

OVERACHIEVER IDEA

Since you'll have chicken bones, can I persuade you to make Overnight Chicken Broth (page 268) in your slow cooker tonight? You'll need some broth for Creamy Chicken and Wild Rice Soup (page 177). Of course you can buy a carton of broth, but wouldn't it be more fun (and healthy and economical!) to make your own?

ITALIAN BEEF TIPS OVER RICE

3 pounds beef round steak or sirloin, cut into ½-inch strips (a **SAVE-IT-FORWARD** item)

2 small bell peppers (mix the colors!), chopped or cut into strips, according to your preference

1 cup sliced mushrooms

One 28-ounce can whole tomatoes, crushed with a wooden spoon or your hands

1 package Lipton Beefy Onion soup mix

2 teaspoons Worcestershire sauce

2 teaspoons minced garlic

1 teaspoon dried basil

Table salt and ground black pepper

Cooked rice, for serving

When I was in my twenties, my mother-in-law, Carolyn, compiled a cookbook called The Family Secrets *that showcased her best recipes. That book was a lifesaver to me when I was a young ninny posing as a bride and mother, and this recipe was one of our favorites. It morphs into another favorite from the book, Mexican Beef Stew, later in the week.*

I've taken some liberties with the original recipe. I don't brown the meat in oil before I add the other ingredients. Shocking! This step would undoubtedly add an extra layer of flavor, but this is Shortcut Week, right? You can just throw all the ingredients into a slow cooker at the same time, and no one will complain about this missing step.

1. Toss the beef, bell pepper, mushrooms, tomatoes, soup mix, Worcestershire, garlic, and basil in the crock of your slow cooker and cook for 6 to 8 hours on low. During the last 30 minutes, remove the lid and turn the temp to high to cook the liquid down a bit. Adjust the seasoning with salt and pepper.

2. Serve over rice. Ahhh, Shortcut Week, you're a home cook's best friend.

SAVE IT FORWARD—BEEF: Reserve 3 cups of the cooked beef for Mexican Beef Stew (page 176). You won't use the sauce, but store it in the sauce for additional flavor.

STROMBOLI

Cooking spray

1 refrigerated pizza crust (I use the kind in a tube in the biscuit section)

⅓ cup jarred Alfredo sauce, plus additional for serving

Freshly ground black pepper

1 cup roughly chopped or shredded rotisserie chicken (see page 171)

1 cup baby spinach

6 slices deli ham

6 slices Swiss cheese (or a mild cheese of your choice)

Italian seasoning (optional, but pretty and tasty)

Strombolis and calzones are first cousins, but a stromboli is rolled in a jelly-roll fashion. I know you're perfectly capable of making your own pizza dough, but during Shortcut Week, I'll be calling you an overachiever if you try that kind of pro move. The refrigerated pizza crust works just fine here!

1. Preheat the oven to 400°F.

2. Spray a sheet pan with cooking spray and unroll the pizza dough. Leave it at about the size it starts out; if you stretch it to be thinner, you'll make holes you'll have to fix. (Overachievers, you can even it out to create a perfect rectangle!)

3. Leaving about 1 inch clear at the edges, slather the dough with the Alfredo sauce and grind some black pepper on top for extra oomph. Add a layer of chicken, then the spinach, ham, and cheese. Starting on a long side, roll the dough up like a jelly roll. Lay it seam side down on the sheet pan, press closed each end to seal the roll, and tuck the ends under the roll.

4. Spray the roll lightly with cooking spray, then sprinkle it lightly with Italian seasoning, if using.

5. Bake for 17 to 20 minutes, until golden brown, starting to check at the 15-minute mark. Lift the roll and make sure it is browned on the bottom before removing it from the oven.

6. If possible, let the stromboli rest for 5 to 10 minutes for cleaner slicing. Cut enough stromboli to serve tonight into 1½-inch slices, leaving the rest intact, and serve.

SAVE IT FORWARD: I have a little trick up my sleeve for the stromboli leftovers, so try to save a bit for a side dish later in the week. See page 179 if you can't wait!

MEXICAN BEEF STEW

2 cups cooked Italian Beef Tips (page 173), saved forward, chopped into bite-size pieces

1 cup prepared salsa, preferably thick and chunky

1 cup small-diced zucchini

One 15-ounce can black beans, rinsed and drained

One 4.5-ounce can chopped green chiles, undrained

¾ cup frozen or canned corn (I use fire-roasted frozen corn)

2 cups chicken broth

Table salt and ground black pepper, to taste

Tortilla chips, sour cream, diced avocado, cilantro, and/or shredded cheese (optional for serving, although I think tortilla chips are essential!)

Here's another recipe from my mother-in-law's Family Secrets *cookbook. Thank you, Carolyn! Her original recipe included cornstarch to make the stew thicker, but we like to serve it brothy with tortilla chips crumbled on top.*

1. This is a great recipe for the Instant Pot! Throw everything in the pot, and set on high pressure for 6 minutes. Do a quick release and you're done! You can also cook this on the stovetop: In a large pot or Dutch oven, combine the beef tips, salsa, zucchini, beans, chiles, corn, broth, and salt and pepper to taste. Bring to a boil, then reduce the heat and simmer, uncovered, for 15 minutes. Adjust the flavor with salt and pepper.

2. Serve the stew with your preferred accompaniments.

CREAMY CHICKEN AND WILD RICE SOUP

1 cup roughly chopped mushrooms

1 cup medium-diced peeled carrots

1 cup medium-diced celery

1 tablespoon olive oil

One 6-ounce box Ben's Original Long Grain and Wild Rice Fast Cook

1 teaspoon minced garlic

6 cups (1½ quarts) Overnight Chicken Broth (page 268) or other chicken broth

2 cups chopped cooked rotisserie chicken (see page 171), saved forward

¼ cup heavy cream (optional but good! See Note on page 178)

The shortcut in this meal is that we're using Ben's Original Long Grain and Wild Rice Fast Cook as the base for the soup. Testimonial: I recently went on a four-day trip, leaving this soup in the fridge so that my homeschooled high schooler would have something to eat for lunch. The kid single-handedly ate the entire batch for four days straight and was disappointed when it was all gone. So, I'd say he liked it!

Oh, and those Toasty Pinwheels (page 179)? Well . . . you cut the leftover stromboli into slices, slather them with a little jarred marinara sauce and cheese, bake for a bit, and give them an imaginative name—your family will be (somewhat) wowed!

1. In a large pot or Dutch oven over medium-low heat, sauté the vegetables in the olive oil until tender, 3 to 5 minutes. Add the rice (reserve the seasoning packet) and sauté for 2 to 3 minutes, until toasted, stirring occasionally. Add the garlic and sauté for 1 or 2 minutes, until fragrant.

2. Add the broth and 2 tablespoons of the seasoning packet. Bring to a boil, then reduce the heat and simmer for 10 minutes. Add the chicken and cream and heat on low until warmed through.

NOTE: Did you know that you can buy tiny cartons of shelf-stable heavy (whipping) cream that are perfect for uses such as this soup? Warning: They don't last forever, so don't hoard them (don't ask me how I know).

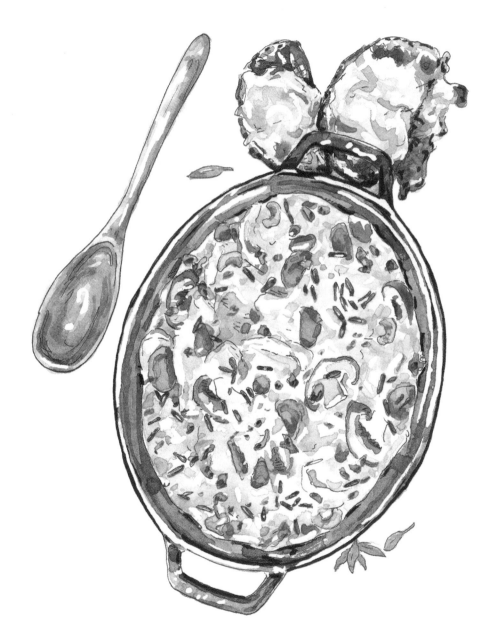

TOASTY PINWHEELS

Stromboli (page 174), saved forward

Cooking spray

Jarred marinara sauce

Grated cheese of your choice

Here's a free mom tip that I've learned over the years: When your family asks you what's for dinner, don't mumble "Leftovers" and look downcast. Make up an imaginative name and announce it cheerily: "Toasty Pinwheels, guys!"

1. Preheat the oven to 400°F.

2. Cut the stromboli loaf into 1½-inch slices. Line a sheet pan with foil, then spray with cooking spray. Place the pinwheels on the foil and bake for 10 minutes, until toasty (hence the name!).

3. Remove the pan from the oven and set the oven to broil. Brush a layer of marinara sauce onto the pinwheels, then top with grated cheese. Broil until the cheese is melted, watching closely so the pinwheels don't burn.

SEARED SCALLOPS with BASIL PESTO CREAM SAUCE AND ORZO

It's honestly shocking how easy this recipe is, but best of all, it looks and tastes as if a professional chef prepared it, even if you're like me and possess zero food-styling skills. Scallops are a tad expensive (particularly when you live on the prairie!), so if you want to skimp on the number of scallops per person, you can supplement with a quick sauté of some shrimp in the same pan. If I'm going to splurge on scallops, I like to buy from a fish market; the frozen ones are often relatively small and tend to get overcooked before you can achieve a nice sear.

This recipe prompted my husband to remember the only time he was paddled at school. His fifth-grade teacher asked, "Does anyone know where scallops come from?" John raised his hand and said, "Scallopian tubes?" And off he went to the principal's office.

Chicken broth (optional)

Scallops, 3 to 4 ounces per person

Table salt

2 cups heavy cream

4 to 5 tablespoons prepared basil pesto

Orzo pasta, as needed to feed your crowd

2 tablespoons butter

Fresh basil leaves (optional)

1. Fill a pasta pot with broth or water (or equal parts) and bring to a boil over high heat. Reduce the heat and cover until you're ready to add the pasta.

2. Rinse the scallops, salt them lightly, and let them drain on paper towels while you're pulling the meal together. Right before cooking, press another paper towel down on top of the scallops to remove all the excess liquid that you can. This will help achieve that professional sear that I promised.

3. In a medium skillet over medium heat, heat the heavy cream until it is bubbly around the edges and has cooked down a bit, 3 to 5 minutes. Whisk 4 tablespoons of the basil pesto into the cream, then taste it to see if you'd like a little more intense flavor. If so, whisk in another tablespoon. Turn off the heat for now, then right before serving, re-warm the sauce. That's it—you made a sauce! I told you it was easy!

4. Bring the broth in the pot back to a boil, add the orzo, cook according to the package directions, and drain.

5. For the scallops, you'll need a skillet large enough to spread the scallops out in that is a good heat conductor, such as cast iron. Heat the pan over medium-high heat. Add the butter to the pan. When sizzling, add the scallops and let them sear undisturbed for about 2 minutes, or until they become opaque about one-third of the way up. Gently lift the tiniest part of one of them to peer at the sear—you're shooting for very brown. When you're happy with the color, carefully flip all the scallops and let them sear undisturbed on the other side until they become opaque one-third of the way up on that side. The whole process will take 4 to 5 minutes. If the scallops are very brown but not entirely done, just turn the heat to low to finish. Don't overcook them!

6. To get that "made by a professional chef" look I've been hyping, spoon a bit of the sauce onto a plate, then nestle the scallops on top of the sauce. Place the orzo creatively on the side, with sauce underneath or drizzled on top—your call. Artfully scatter a few basil leaves around, if you got 'em. Alternatively, you could mix the sauce into the orzo as a bed for the scallops, scattering slivers of fresh basil on top.

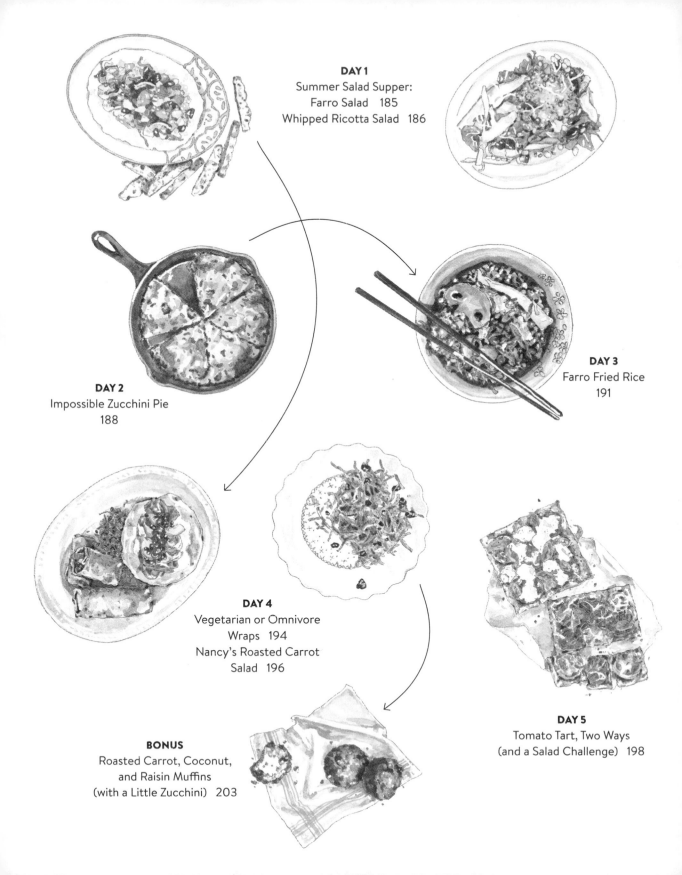

Veggie-Forward Week, Spring-Summer Edition

Ahh, the joys of summer veggies! I hope you like tomatoes and zucchini, because they'll be your friends this week. Even if you don't, you can still find some meals to love, with a bonus muffin to launch your weekend with a tasty (and healthy!) start.

SUMMER SALAD SUPPER

Our friends the Sullivans are both healthy eaters and adventuresome, so they were the perfect victims for a recipe-testing dinner party. These two salads on platters made a gorgeous spread, and I hope they inspire you to invite a healthy, adventuresome friend to dinner around your table!

ADVANCE PREP

You can leisurely make most of these components on the weekend, then assemble on another day for a super-quick meal. The ricotta is the one exception; I would whip it right before serving.

FARRO SALAD

This salad was inspired by my favorite salad from Zoës Kitchen restaurants, but they broke my heart and discontinued it—unforgivable. I re-created it in my home kitchen, though, so my soul has regained its equilibrium.

¼ cup Everyday Vinaigrette (page 269) or bottled vinaigrette, plus more for serving

1 tablespoon prepared basil pesto

¼ teaspoon crushed red pepper flakes

1 pound farro, cooked and cooled (a **SAVE-IT-FORWARD** item; see Note)

1 medium zucchini, cut into very thin lengthwise "ribbons" (see Note)

1 medium yellow squash, cut into very thin lengthwise "ribbons" (see Note)

2 cups or handfuls baby spinach

1 cup medium-diced tomatoes (I use halved cherry tomatoes if I can't get homegrown)

2 cups edamame beans (see Note)

¼ cup grated Parmesan, for serving

1. In a medium bowl, whisk the Everyday Vinaigrette, pesto, and red pepper flakes. Add 2 cups of the farro and toss to combine.

2. On a platter or large serving dish, toss the zucchini, yellow squash, spinach, tomatoes, and edamame. Add a light amount of the vinaigrette mixture and toss again. Make a space in the middle of the veggies for a mound of the farro mixture. Sprinkle with Parmesan and serve.

SAVE IT FORWARD—FARRO: You'll need about 5 cups cooked farro for the Farro Fried Rice (page 191), depending on your family size.

NOTE ON FARRO: I hesitate to give any cooking directions for farro because they would depend on what brand you can find at your grocery store. I found a quick-cooking variety at Trader Joe's during one of my occasional pilgrimages. I cooked it in vegetable broth, but water (or chicken broth) works, too.

NOTE ON SQUASH: I used a vegetable peeler to make long, thin ribbons. I bet a mandoline would work, too, but I didn't want to drag mine out.

NOTE ON EDAMAME: You're going to have a decision to make, based on your budget and time. You'll find edamame in both pod and bean form in the freezer aisle. If you buy the pods, you'll have to pop the beans out of the pods. I tasked the Sullivans with this—I like to put my guests to work! It's not difficult, but next time I'll probably buy just the beans.

WHIPPED RICOTTA SALAD

One 15-ounce container whole milk ricotta

Table salt

1½ cups large-diced tomatoes (if you can't find homegrown, I'd use halved cherry tomatoes)

1 cup large-diced peeled cucumber

¼ cup red onion slivers

⅛ cup small fresh basil leaves or thinly cut basil

2 tablespoons Everyday Vinaigrette (page 269) or bottled vinaigrette, plus more to taste

Ground black pepper

Grilled or toasted French or Italian bread, for serving

Honey, for serving (optional)

Guys! This salad is delicious and gorgeous—I hope you make it! It's great on toasted or grilled bread, piled high with the fluffy ricotta and tangy veggies. A crusty Italian bread is perfect, particularly brushed with a little olive oil and rubbed with a garlic clove. At my outpost on the prairie, I can't find crusty bread, so I just buttered and toasted some dinner rolls, and they were great, too.

1. In a food processor or mixer, blend the ricotta and ¾ teaspoon salt until light and fluffy, 3 to 4 minutes. Spread the ricotta out on a platter.

2. In a medium bowl, combine the tomatoes, cucumber, onion, basil, and vinaigrette. Taste the mixture and add more vinaigrette and salt and pepper as desired.

3. Spread the veggie mixture over the ricotta, leaving a margin of ricotta around the edges for a beautiful presentation.

4. Serve with grilled or toasted bread and a drizzle of honey, if you are feeling adventurous.

SAVE IT FORWARD—WHIPPED RICOTTA SALAD: If you have any leftover salad, save it for the Vegetarian or Omnivore Wraps (page 194)!

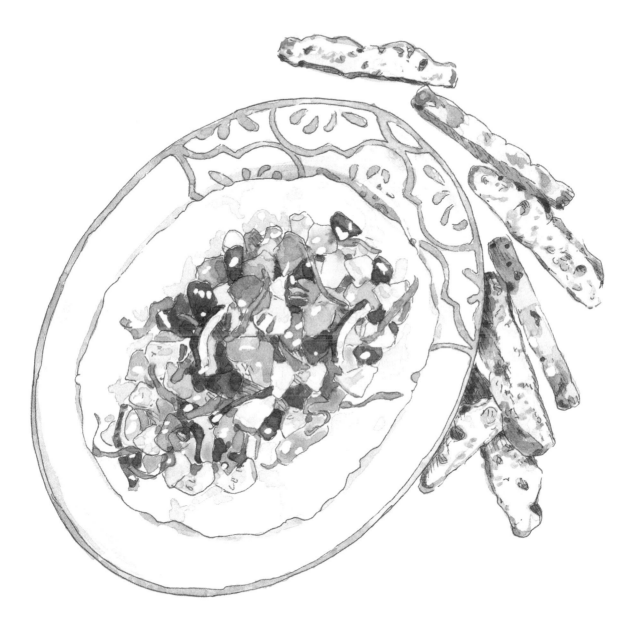

IMPOSSIBLE ZUCCHINI PIE

Cooking spray

3 cups shredded zucchini (a **SAVE-IT-FORWARD** item)

½ teaspoon table salt

4 large eggs

1 cup baking mix (such as Bisquick)

½ cup cottage cheese or sour cream

1 tablespoon olive or vegetable oil

1½ cups grated cheese of your choice (I use 1 cup cheddar and ½ cup Parmesan)

½ teaspoon Italian seasoning

½ teaspoon garlic powder

½ teaspoon ground black pepper

1 cup finely chopped yellow onion

1 cup shredded carrots (a **SAVE-IT-FORWARD** item; I buy bagged)

If you didn't grow up in the 1960s and '70s, you might have missed the Impossible Pie trend, when Bisquick was the apple of every homemaker's eye, including my mom's. I want to launch a one-woman movement to #BringBackImpossiblePies! They're honestly really good, and (Bis)QUICK. Healthwise, Impossible Pies are not terribly carb-laden, since you use just one cup of the baking mix in the entire recipe, and there are also gluten-free and heart-healthy versions of Bisquick available nowadays. If you're a purist, you can make your own baking mix, particularly if you have self-rising flour on hand from pizza night, and I bet you could even sub pancake mix. Can you tell I'm giving you no excuses to not try this?! In terms of veggies, this recipe is very flexible: substitute any combination of vegetables you like.

1. Preheat the oven to 350°F. Spray a 12-inch pie pan or a 6 x 10-inch baking dish with cooking spray.

2. Spread the zucchini on paper towels and sprinkle with the salt.

3. In a large bowl, whisk the eggs. Add the baking mix, cottage cheese or sour cream, oil, cheese, Italian seasoning, garlic powder, and pepper. Mix until just combined.

4. Press down on the zucchini with more paper towels to remove as much of the liquid as you can. Add the zucchini, onion, and carrots to the bowl and mix just until combined.

5. Pour the mixture into the greased pan and bake for 40 to 45 minutes, until the pie is golden brown and set in the middle. If you can beat back your hungry eaters, let the pie sit for 10 to 15 minutes to cool and firm up a bit.

SAVE IT FORWARD—ZUCCHINI AND CARROTS: In case you're pulling out the food processor for a shredding extravaganza, here are the total amounts of zucchini and carrots you'll need for the week.

- **ZUCCHINI:** You'll need 5 cups of shredded zucchini, or 3 to 4 medium zucchini.

- **CARROTS:** If you cook everything in this week's menu, you'll need 9½ cups of shredded carrots (hello, beta carotene!). If you're buying the matchstick carrots from the produce aisle, you'll need 3 bags; each 10-ounce bag contains 4 cups (you'll have a little extra to add to various dishes this week).

**LUNCH BITS
AND BOBS:**

*Leftover Impossible
Zucchini Pie is
delightful warmed up
for lunch! It's great at
room temperature or
cold, too.*

NOTE ON SHREDDED CARROTS: Little did I know the difference between shredded and grated-at-home carrots until I started tinkering with this recipe. I started by grating carrots myself on a box grater, and the results were lackluster. Meanwhile, my recipe tester, Brandi, was tinkering, too, and she told me about the shredded (aka matchstick) carrots you can buy in a bag. Eureka! I suppose you industrious types can shred the carrots in your food processor, but I gotta say . . . those shredded carrots from the produce aisle are just fine and not expensive.

FARRO FRIED RICE

3 tablespoons sesame oil (or vegetable or olive oil, though not as flavorful)

5 cups cooked farro (see page 185), saved forward

2 cups broccoli florets

1 cup diced or sliced yellow onion

2 cups sliced mushrooms (I use baby portobellos—delicious!)

1 cup frozen peas (throw them in frozen!)

½ cup shredded zucchini (see page 189), saved forward

½ cup shredded carrots (see page 189), saved forward

2 garlic cloves, minced

3 eggs

¼ cup low-sodium soy sauce (less if you're using the full-sodium version), plus more for serving

Sriracha, for serving (optional)

I may love chewy, toothy Farro Fried Rice better than the white rice version! This is a complete meal: farro is a high-protein grain, and the eggs add protein. The vegetables here are very flexible; see the Note on page 193 for some shortcuts if you're pressed for time. And if you'd like to add meat or seafood, feel free to go rogue on my Veggie Week theme. I generally serve this rice with some sort of fruit, but if a gas station egg roll sounds tasty, no judgment here!

NOTE: This dish comes together quickly, so be sure to have all the ingredients on hand and measured out before you start!

1. In a deep pan or wok, heat 2 tablespoons of the sesame oil over medium heat until a grain of farro sizzles when added to the pan. Add the farro, broccoli, and onions and cook until the vegetables start to become tender, stirring frequently, about 3 minutes.

2. Make a well in the middle of the pan and add the remaining 1 tablespoon of the sesame oil. Heat until sizzling. Add the mushrooms, peas, zucchini, and carrots, stirring frequently and cooking until the veggies are tender, about 3 minutes. Have a cup of water next to the stove, and if the veggies start to stick, add a couple of tablespoons at a time and continue stirring. Add the garlic and cook until fragrant, about 1 minute.

TO DO TONIGHT:

If you have extra time tonight, make Nancy's Roasted Carrot Salad (page 196), which benefits from the flavors melding overnight. It's also fine to make it right before mealtime.

3. Make a well again in the middle of the pan. Turn the heat to medium-low and crack the eggs into the well and scramble them by stirring them continuously until they are set. Turn off the heat, then incorporate them into the vegetable and farro mixture. Add the soy sauce and stir gently until combined.

4. If you like a little heat (I do!), add some sriracha for serving, as well as more soy sauce.

NOTE ON VEGGIES: The veggie choices here are very flexible; just use 7 total cups of vegetables. If your family likes mushrooms, they do add a nice meatiness to this meatless meal. If you don't already have grated zucchini and carrots saved forward from previous meals, sub out something less labor-intensive. I'll often use a bag of frozen mixed vegetables, such as the variety with peas, carrots, corn, and green beans. Microwave them briefly to thaw—they work like a charm and save time and money.

VEGETARIAN OR OMNIVORE WRAPS

These wraps and Nancy's Roasted Carrot Salad (page 196) make the simplest of meals, which might even give you a little extra time to bake the weekend's muffins (see page 203) tonight if you're feeling industrious. In keeping with the Veggie-Forward Week theme, I didn't officially add any meat to this recipe, but if you happen to have a rotisserie chicken in the fridge, some roast chicken would be a great addition.

The amounts here are not exact but depend on how many tortillas you're making:

Flour tortillas (or brown rice or low-carb tortillas)

Laughing Cow cheese, one wedge per tortilla (or sub cream cheese)

Whipped Ricotta Salad (page 186), including the veggies, saved forward

Raw spinach, stemmed

One 15-ounce can seasoned black beans, drained

Avocado, sliced

Rotisserie chicken slices (optional)

Table salt and ground black pepper

Salsa, for serving (optional)

1. Warm the tortillas in the microwave for a few seconds to make them pliable.

2. Spread a wedge of Laughing Cow cheese (or a bit of cream cheese) on each tortilla. Add a schmear of the whipped ricotta and the accompanying veggies, then layer on the spinach, beans, avocado, and chicken, if using. Season with salt and pepper to taste and wrap like a burrito.

3. Serve with salsa, if desired.

NANCY'S ROASTED CARROT SALAD

Two 10-ounce bags shredded carrots (see page 190)

2 tablespoons olive oil

1 teaspoon table salt

4 tablespoons honey or agave

2 cups shredded unsweetened coconut (sweetened works, too!)

2 cups raisins (I used a berry blend because that's all I had, and it was great!)

¼ cup freshly squeezed lemon juice

True confession: I had never eaten a carrot salad when I tried this recipe for the cookbook. I never saw the point—just eat a carrot, I thought! I was remarkably uninterested in adding a glop of mayonnaise to a bowl of carrots. Then I got a text from my beloved Nancy, a cousin by marriage and a sister by heart. She knew that my cookbook was all about saving things forward, so she reimagined her (non-gloppy!) carrot salad into carrot, coconut, and raisin muffins (see page 203)—genius! If you don't want to make the muffins, you may want to halve this recipe, though the salad does keep well for a week of nibbling.

1. Preheat the oven to 400°F. Cover 2 sheet pans with foil.

2. In a large bowl, mix the carrots, olive oil, salt, and 2 tablespoons of the honey.

3. Divide the mixture between the sheet pans and roast for 5 minutes. (Set the bowl aside.)

4. Add 1 cup of the shredded coconut and 1 tablespoon of the honey to each of the pans and stir to combine. Roast until the carrots and coconut start to brown, about 20 minutes.

5. Use a spatula to transfer the carrot mixture from each pan back to the bowl. Add the raisins and lemon juice and toss to combine. Refrigerate until serving.

6. The salad can be served cold or at room temperature. If you make it ahead and it becomes a tad dry, just sprinkle a few drops of water over it and stir before serving.

SAVE IT FORWARD—ROASTED CARROT SALAD: Save 1 to 2 cups of this salad to use in Roasted Carrot, Coconut, and Raisin Muffins (with a Little Zucchini), page 203, depending on the size of the batch you want to make.

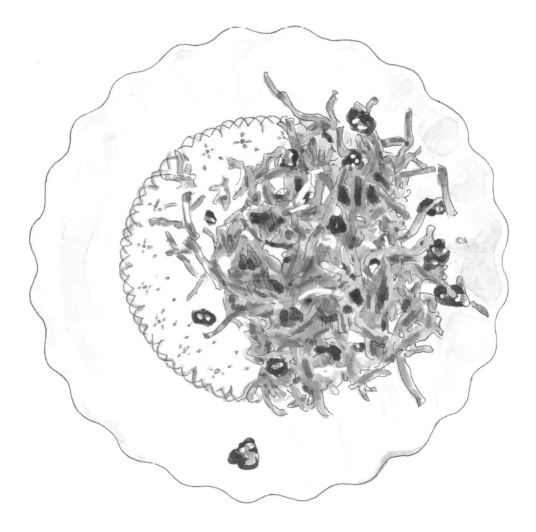

TOMATO TART, TWO WAYS (AND A SALAD CHALLENGE)

TOMATO TART, CHEESY VERSION

1 frozen Pepperidge Farm puff pastry sheet

1 large homegrown tomato

Table salt

¼ cup mayonnaise (I'm a Duke's mayo girl myself)

½ to ¾ of one 8-ounce ball fresh mozzarella, sliced thin

Fresh or dried herbs of your choice (I had some thyme in my fridge, so I used that)

¾ cup freshly grated Parmesan

I recently made this tart for a girlfriend's birthday dinner and paired it with a vinaigrette-y green salad with grilled chicken. Oh, and daiquiris. The meal got rave reviews, and I don't think it was just the daiquiris talking! The key to the success of this recipe is homegrown tomatoes. Though I don't grow my own, in summer I can always track down a friend with a bumper crop, thanks to Facebook.

I created two versions of this tart, and it was fun (and pretty!) to have two different taste sensations. The first is a melted cheesy delight, and the second one has very little cheese (or you can skip it entirely). Both are wonderful!

Each uses one frozen Pepperidge Farm puff pastry sheet, which come two to a package. If you haven't yet discovered the magic of puff pastry, it's amazing—no other kitchen shortcut has a better fancy-yet-easy ratio. Give it a whirl!

1. Preheat the oven to 400°F. You'll need two racks placed in the middle part of the oven, and they can be close together.

2. Thirty minutes before you assemble the tarts, remove the puff pastry sheets from the freezer. Don't take them out much earlier because they will defrost too soon and become difficult to unroll.

3. Thinly slice the tomatoes for both tarts, salt them lightly, lay the slices on paper towels, and cover with another layer of paper towels. This step is crucial to keep the tarts from being too watery.

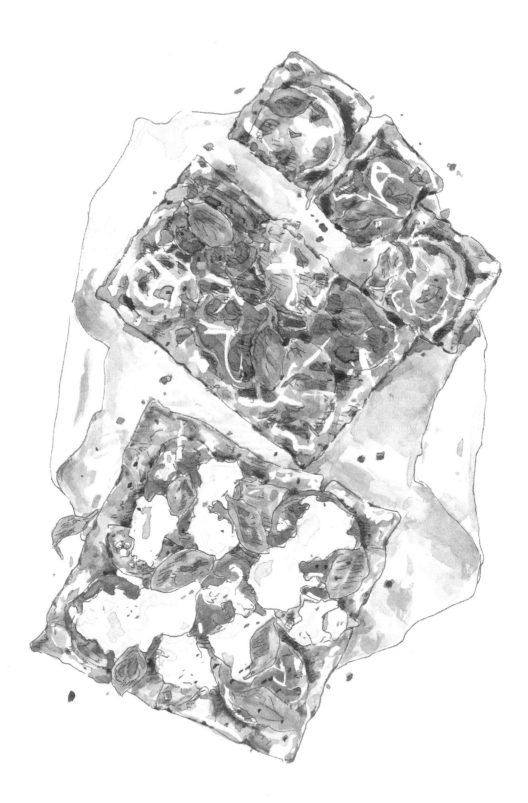

TOMATO TART, HUMMUS AND PESTO VERSION

1 frozen Pepperidge Farm puff pastry sheet

1 large homegrown tomato

Table salt

¼ cup Hummus (page 209) or purchased (see Note)

¼ cup prepared basil pesto (from a jar or your garden!)

2 tablespoons thinly sliced fresh basil leaves

½ cup freshly grated Parmesan (optional)

4. Unroll each puff pastry sheet onto a sheet pan and prick the dough every couple of inches with a fork. Throw them back in the freezer for a bit if they are sticky and aren't unrolling easily.

5. To assemble the first tart, slather one of the puff pastry sheets with a mayonnaise layer (leaving about 1 inch bare at the edges), then cover the mayo with a single tomato layer. Place a thin slice of fresh mozzarella on each tomato slice. Sprinkle with the herbs and Parmesan.

6. To assemble the second tart, slather the other puff pastry sheet with a layer of the hummus (leaving about 1 inch bare at the edges), then a layer of the pesto. Cover the pesto with a single tomato layer. Sprinkle the fresh basil and Parmesan, if using, over the tomatoes.

7. Set the sheet pans on different oven racks and bake the tarts for 25 to 30 minutes, until they are very golden brown on the bottom (lift the edge of a tart to confirm).

8. Slice, serve, and revel in your fanciness!

NOTE ON HUMMUS: Of course you can buy prepared hummus, but if you're planning ahead for next week's Mediterranean Week menu, you could make the hummus now and save it forward for next week.

SALAD CHALLENGE: *You probably have a bunch of veggie bits and bobs lurking in your fridge, and possibly even some vinaigrette and cooked farro. I challenge you to throw it all together in a pretty bowl and see what sort of delicious alchemy emerges!*

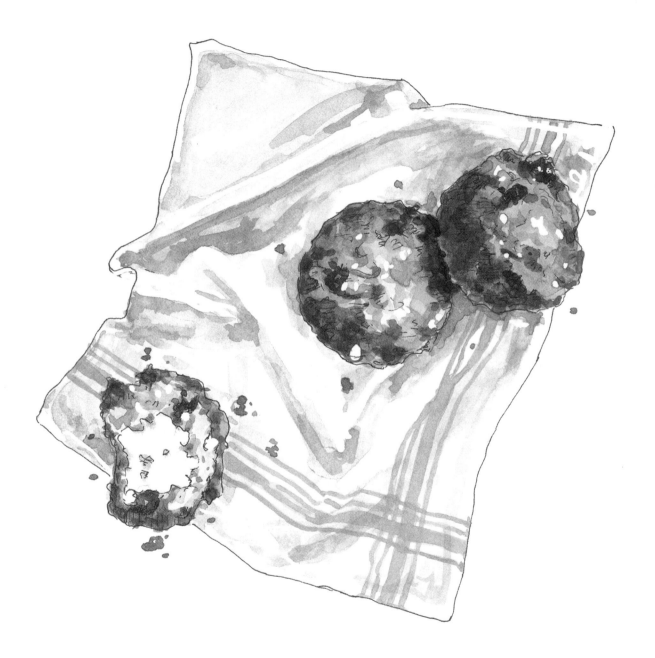

ROASTED CARROT, COCONUT, AND RAISIN MUFFINS (WITH A LITTLE ZUCCHINI)

Cooking spray

2 cups Nancy's Roasted Carrot Salad (page 196), saved forward

1½ cups shredded zucchini

½ cup chopped pecans or walnuts (optional, but delicious)

Zest of 1 orange (optional)

½ cup freshly squeezed orange juice (or prepared orange juice)

2 eggs

½ cup vegetable oil or melted coconut oil (I use refined coconut oil to diminish the coconut flavor)

½ cup sugar

2 teaspoons vanilla extract

2 cups Bisquick

Turbinado (raw) sugar, for sprinkling (optional)

Thank you to my cousin Nancy for this ingenious idea of morphing her carrot salad into muffins! I felt downright virtuous eating muffins packed full of such healthy ingredients. This recipe will make twelve muffins, so just halve the recipe if that's too many (though they freeze well), or if you didn't have two cups of the carrot salad to save forward.

1. Preheat the oven to 350°F. Spray a large muffin pan with cooking spray.

2. In a large bowl, combine the carrot salad, zucchini, pecans, orange zest (if using), orange juice, eggs, oil, sugar, and vanilla. Mix well. Add the Bisquick and mix just until combined.

3. Divide the batter among the pan wells (it's fine to fill to the top since they don't rise much). If you want to take these muffins to the next level, sprinkle the tops with turbinado sugar for a little sparkle.

4. Bake for 19 to 24 minutes, until browned around the edges and firm in the middle.

5. Though it is tempting to eat these warm from the oven, it's best to let them cool and firm up a bit. Ignore me if you don't mind a messy muffin!

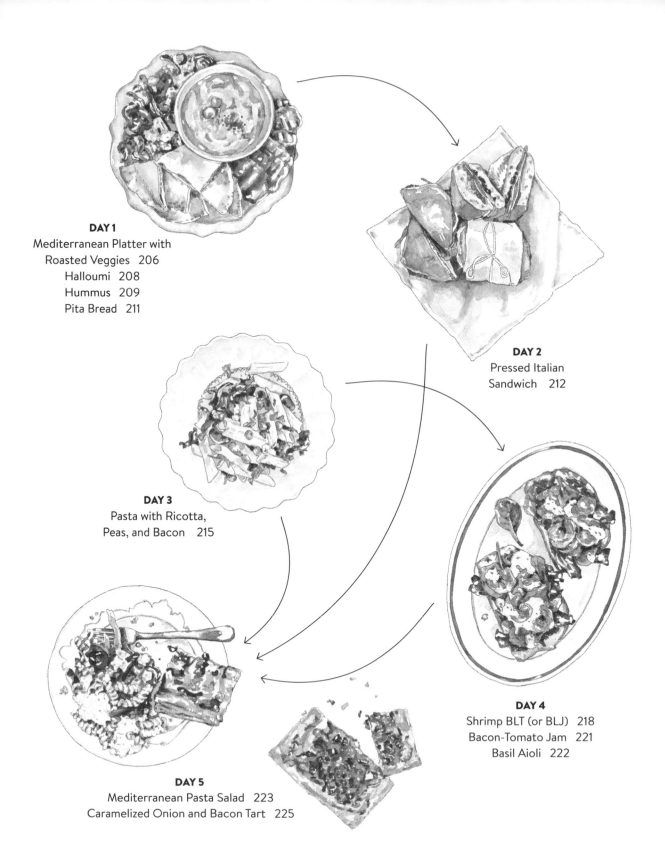

Mediterranean Week

Mediterranean cuisine is my favorite because it celebrates that magical marriage of olive oil, bread, cheese, pasta, vegetables, and basil. Since my husband is a gluten-free guy, I use gluten-free pasta and bread in these recipes (though I sometimes eat the glutinous stuff when he's not around). This week we use some Mediterranean specialty foods such as olive tapenade and sun-dried tomatoes, but we use them twice, to be thrifty!

ADVANCE PREP

If you want to get a head start on your week, make these components ahead of time so that the rest of the week is more about assembling meals than cooking:

- Roasted veggies (see page 206)
- Hummus (page 209)—you'll have plenty of extra for nibbling!
- Basil Aioli (page 222)—it will last for a good long time.
- Bacon (see page 217)—cook a pound (or two, depending on how many people you're feeding), reserving 4 tablespoons of bacon grease for the pasta dish.
- Bacon-Tomato Jam (page 221)—this takes Shrimp BLTs to the next level, and it's a great use for the bacon you're already making. No canning required!
- Caramelized onions (see page 227)—my shortcut version using the slow cooker is completely hands-off!
- Crème Fraîche (page 226)—this is another almost completely hands-off recipe, though crème fraîche does need at least 48 hours of sitting around. It lasts for several days in the fridge, and it's used in Week 14, Veggie-Forward Week, Fall-Winter Edition (page 229), as well, if you're cooking the weeks in order.

MEDITERRANEAN PLATTER with ROASTED VEGGIES, HALLOUMI, HUMMUS, and PITA BREAD

¼ cup olive oil

1 tablespoon maple syrup (or pancake syrup)

2 teaspoons seasoned salt blend (I use Lawry's Seasoned Salt)

2 teaspoons garlic powder

¼ teaspoon crushed red pepper flakes

16 ounces mushrooms, cut into medium slices

1 head cauliflower, cut into small florets

1 zucchini, cut into ½-inch half-moons

1 medium red onion, cut into ½-inch slivers

Halloumi (recipe follows)

Hummus (recipe follows)

Pita Bread (recipe follows), cut into triangles, for serving

I made a spread of these terrific components and arranged them on one big serving platter—a feast for the eyes and palate!

To compose the meal, arrange the roasted veggies in sections on the platter. Snuggle the cooked Halloumi cheese in with the veggies. Nestle the bowl of hummus in the middle of the veggies. Arrange the pita triangles around the other items. Dive in—you've created a Mediterranean masterpiece.

1. Preheat the oven to 400°F. Cover 2 sheet pans with foil.

2. In a small bowl, whisk the olive oil, maple syrup, seasoned salt, garlic powder, and red pepper flakes.

3. Keeping the vegetables separated by type, spread the mushrooms, cauliflower, zucchini, and onion on the sheet pans in a (mostly) single layer. Toss the veggies with the olive oil mixture, still keeping them within their little sections.

4. Roast the vegetables for approximately 40 minutes, until delightfully browned and caramelized, though some veggies may take a little more or less time (feel free to remove veggies as they finish roasting).

5. Serve with Halloumi, hummus, and pita triangles.

SAVE IT FORWARD—VEGGIES: You can add the leftover veggies to the Pressed Italian Sandwich on page 212!

HALLOUMI

1 block Halloumi cheese,
cut into ¼-inch slices

Olive oil

Over the last couple of years, I would read with longing the gleeful crowing from the coast-dwellers about this mystical cheese that the fancy people were grilling. What? I stalked specialty stores in Tulsa for months until one blessed day, the heavens parted and Halloumi landed at the cheese counter. What is this cheese that warrants this compulsive behavior, you ask? By definition, Halloumi is a semi-hard cheese made from goat, sheep or cow's milk; originally from Cyprus. Here's the magical part, though: Halloumi holds its shape and texture well when grilled or fried. Bottom line: it's worth the trek into the big city, my rural friends! But, if you can't find Halloumi or order it, serve the cheese of your choice.

Brush the Halloumi slices with a bit of oil. Heat a grill pan or nonstick pan over medium heat. Add the Halloumi and cook for 2 to 3 minutes per side, until nicely browned.

HUMMUS

One 16-ounce can chickpeas, rinsed

½ teaspoon baking soda

½ cup freshly squeezed lemon juice, plus more to taste

2 garlic cloves

1 teaspoon table salt, plus more to taste

1 cup tahini

About ¼ cup ice water

2 tablespoons olive oil, plus more for serving if desired

¾ teaspoon ground cumin

½ teaspoon paprika, plus more for serving if desired

Hummus is surprisingly easy to make, and cheap compared with the store-bought varieties. I've been on a quest to make really smooth hummus, and I've tested a few methods. The first method worked but was quite tedious because it involved squeezing the skin off every dang chickpea. Um, no. Who has time for that? The technique I like best involves cooking canned chickpeas with some baking soda, which removes most of the skins for you! I cooked mine in an Instant Pot, but you can also simmer them on the stove. I'm always looking for a shortcut, but to save even more money, you could cook dried chickpeas instead of using canned.

1. To cook the chickpeas in an Instant Pot, combine them and the baking soda in the pot with a chickpea can of water. Cook for 11 minutes at high pressure and do a quick release. Rinse with cold water. Many of the skins will be loose, so remove all that you can easily pull off.

2. To cook the chickpeas on the stove, combine them in a medium saucepan with the baking soda and a chickpea can of water. Bring to a boil over medium-high heat, lower the heat to a simmer, and cook for 20 minutes. Rinse with cold water. Many of the skins will be loose, so remove all that you can easily pull off.

3. In the bowl of a food processor or in a high-speed blender, combine the lemon juice, garlic, and salt.

Blend well, then let the mixture sit for 5 to 10 minutes to mellow the garlic. Add the tahini and blend well, adding 3 tablespoons of the ice water as you process.

4. Add the chickpeas and olive oil and process until the mixture becomes smooth and light in color. This might take several minutes. Add the cumin and paprika and process until combined. Test to see if the hummus is creamy; if not, add more ice water, a tablespoon at a time. Taste to see if the hummus needs more zing, and add more salt or lemon as desired.

5. Place the hummus in a nice serving bowl. Serve with a drizzle of olive oil and/or a sprinkle of paprika over the top if you like!

LUNCH BITS AND BOBS

You'll likely have a lot of hummus left over, which is always good news in my household! Obviously, I don't need to tell you to eat it with tortilla chips or crackers, but I thought I'd mention a few less obvious uses:

FLATBREAD PIZZA: Brush a pita with a little olive oil and bake at 400°F for about 5 minutes. Spread with a layer of hummus, then top with a quick Greek salad: arugula or spinach, tomatoes, olives, lemon juice, olive oil, feta, salt, and pepper.

DEVILED EGGS: Mash the yolk of a hard-boiled egg with some hummus, possibly adding a little bit of mayo if too dry. Spoon the mixture back into the hard-boiled egg white halves and sprinkle with a little paprika.

SALMON PATTY TACOS: My daughter, Meg, discovered that a salmon patty makes a great taco filling with a schmear of hummus (page 159). Or, create a vegetarian taco with hummus and lots of fresh veggies.

PITA BREAD

You didn't think I would give you a recipe for actually making pita bread from scratch, did you? Heck, no—wrong girl! I completely support and applaud you if you want to do that—but here I'll just give you a few options for warming up pita bread.

1. Wrap a pita bread in foil and stick it in the oven at 350°F for about 10 minutes.

2. Wrap a pita bread in a damp paper towel and microwave it for 20 seconds or so.

3. If you have a gas stove, set it to a medium-low flame and hold a pita bread over the flame with a pair of tongs for a few seconds. When one side gets lightly browned, flip it, and warm the other side. This technique will even work on frozen pitas!

PRESSED ITALIAN SANDWICH

Ciabatta rolls or loaves, or a sturdy, thick-crusted bread

Olive oil

Olive tapenade (a **SAVE-IT-FORWARD** item) or finely chopped olives

Sun-dried tomatoes (either dry or oil-packed; a **SAVE-IT-FORWARD** item), diced

Sliced deli ham (or meat of your choice)

Sliced provolone cheese

Fresh greens such as arugula and basil leaves or spinach (a **SAVE-IT-FORWARD** item)

Roasted veggies (see page 206), saved forward (optional)

Sliced deli pepperoni or Italian salami (a **SAVE-IT-FORWARD** item)

In my obsession with all things Italian, I've read about this sandwich, allegedly what Italians bring on charming picnics, undoubtedly alongside a bottle of red wine. The skeptical side of me wonders if they really do this, or is it just an American fantasy? (Do people imagine that ranch cowboys still eat from chuckwagons? Pickup tailgates, for sure!)

I went all out in terms of fun and frivolous ingredients on this sandwich, but to be honest it was way too fancy for the sixteen-year-old caveman I'm raising. He wanted meat and cheese, period. No olive tapenade! No arugula and basil! No sun-dried tomatoes! Oh, and he wanted his sandwich heated in the microwave. Doesn't he know that there are no microwaves on Italian countryside picnics? Sheesh. So, if you're raising a caveman, you might let him construct his own dang sandwich for the sake of family harmony.

I don't list quantities for this recipe, as they're easily adjusted to however many people you are feeding. Pair these sandwiches with chips and fruit and make yourself a picnic! Of course, throwing a blanket down at a picturesque spot would be the most fun, but if that's too ambitious, just plop everyone on the floor and call it an indoor picnic—whatever works for you!

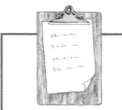

TO DO TONIGHT:
*If you're making
homemade Crème
Fraîche (page 226)
for the Caramelized
Onion and Bacon
Tart (page 225), start
it tonight. It will take
just 5 minutes of
prep, and you'll feel
like a boss.*

1. Cut the rolls in half and remove some of the inner bread so that the sandwiches will be less dense. (See Save It Forward—Miscellaneous below.)

2. For each sandwich, brush the inside of one roll half with olive oil. Spread the tapenade on the inside of the other roll half and add a sprinkling of sun-dried tomatoes. Add a couple of ham layers, a layer of cheese, a layer of arugula and basil leaves, a thin layer of the leftover roasted veggies (if using), another layer of cheese, and the pepperoni. Top with the other half of the roll.

3. Wrap each sandwich with plastic wrap, making sure that it is entirely wrapped, even the ends. Set the sandwiches in the refrigerator and top them with something heavy; I use a cast-iron skillet filled with heavy cans. You could also stack cans on a heavy cutting board. Refrigerate the pressed sandwiches for at least 4 hours to overnight (or even longer).

4. Cut into slices to serve. My son will feel vindicated if you choose to heat yours a bit, in either the oven or microwave, but the rest of us like these cold!

SAVE IT FORWARD—MISCELLANEOUS: More olive tapenade, sun-dried tomatoes, and pepperoni will be used later in the week in Mediterranean Pasta Salad (page 223). Save the bread scraps, too. Sauté them in olive oil or butter until they are almost crunchy, then crumble them and use as bread crumbs, if desired.

SAVE IT FORWARD—ARUGULA: Use any extra arugula for a salad to go with the pasta tomorrow night.

PASTA WITH RICOTTA, PEAS, AND BACON

6 bacon slices

Penne or rotini pasta (see Save It Forward—Pasta on page 216 for quantity; a **SAVE-IT-FORWARD** item)

Table salt, for the pasta water, plus more to taste

6 ounces frozen peas (about 1 cup)

One 15-ounce carton ricotta

2 tablespoons butter, at room temperature

4-ounce log of chèvre (goat cheese), crumbled into small chunks (see Note on Substitution on page 216)

½ cup freshly grated Parmesan, plus more for serving

Freshly ground black pepper

This recipe is a riff on a Marcella Hazan recipe, and like most of her recipes, the genius is in its simplicity. Accordingly, a simple salad with saved-forward arugula, lemon juice, and Parmesan is all you need to round out this lovely dish. God rest your soul, Marcella, for introducing Americans (particularly me!) to your beloved Italian cuisine.

1. Cook the bacon (see Save It Forward—Bacon on page 217), reserving 4 tablespoons of bacon grease. Roughly chop the bacon and set it aside.

2. Fill a pasta pot with water and plenty of salt—it should taste like the sea!—and bring it to a boil. Cook the pasta according to the al dente package directions, reserve 2 cups of the pasta water (very important!), drain the pasta, and return it to the pot. If you're cooking extra pasta for the pasta salad, set some aside and refrigerate it.

3. In a skillet on medium-low heat, cook the frozen peas with the reserved bacon grease until the peas are thawed. Add the chopped bacon and cook until the peas and bacon are warmed.

4. Whip the ricotta and butter until fluffy. I use a hand mixer and whip it in the serving dish.

5. To assemble, add the drained pasta to the serving dish with the ricotta mixture and the chèvre, and toss until the chèvre is melted and incorporated into the pasta. Add the bacon, peas, and Parmesan to the pasta and stir to combine. Add the reserved pasta water a little at a time—probably at least 1 cup—until the pasta is flavorful and moist. Add salt and freshly ground pepper to taste.

6. Divide the pasta among individual bowls and sprinkle with more freshly grated Parmesan and serve.

NOTE ON SUBSTITUTION: If you are not a fan of chèvre you can substitute a bit of heavy cream or cream cheese, enough to make the dish a bit more creamy.

SAVE IT FORWARD—PASTA: If you're cooking only enough for this dish, allow 2 to 3 ounces of dry pasta per person. If you're serving Mediterranean Pasta Salad (page 223) later in the week, add 12 more ounces to the pot.

TO DO TONIGHT:
If you haven't already made Bacon-Tomato Jam (page 221) for tomorrow night's Shrimp BLTs, you might want to do it tonight, since it needs to cook for 30 to 45 minutes. You could also make the Basil Aioli while it cooks, and tomorrow's dinner will be a breeze!

SAVE IT FORWARD—BACON: The day I learned from a savvy homeschooling friend how to cook bacon in the oven, the heavens parted and I heard angels singing. Give it a try! To make 1 pound of bacon, line 2 sheet pans with extra-wide foil, which will keep the bacon grease from leaking through to the pan. Place the bacon slices side by side on the pans, without overlapping them. Bake at 400°F for 30 minutes or longer, depending on the thickness of the bacon. You'll likely need to rotate the pans to a different rack halfway through the cooking time. Remove the bacon when it is just starting to brown but not yet crispy. Drain on paper towels. For this recipe, scoop out 4 tablespoons of bacon grease before you discard the foil.

There are four possible bacon uses this week: this pasta dish, the BLT on page 218 along with the accompanying Bacon-Tomato Jam (page 221), and the Caramelized Onion and Bacon Tart on page 225. If you plan on making all four dishes, cook at least a pound of bacon, possibly 1½ pounds (which will require another sheet pan or a second round of cooking).

SHRIMP BLT (OR BLJ) with BACON-TOMATO JAM and BASIL AIOLI

Sturdy bread of your choice (these sandwiches are open-faced, so one slice is needed per sandwich)

Butter, softened (optional)

Bacon-Tomato Jam (recipe follows) or jam of your choice

1½ cooked bacon slices per sandwich (see page 217), saved forward, warmed

Lettuce or spinach leaves

2 to 4 cooked medium shrimp per sandwich, depending on the size (see Note on page 220)

Basil Aioli (optional but spectacular; recipe follows; a **SAVE-IT-FORWARD** item)

My daughter, Meg, and her husband, Stephen, came home from a trip to California raving about this restaurant dish, so they re-created it for me. Wow! The original version used tomato jam, which I couldn't find (well, not at a price I was willing to pay), so Brandi, my recipe tester, created a bacon-tomato jam for us. Again—wow! It's a fresh jam that stays in the fridge, so there's no canning necessary. I also tested this recipe with some jalapeño jelly I had stashed in my pantry, and that was tasty, too. I think a thin layer of almost any jam could work: maybe an orange marmalade, or apricot or strawberry jam with some added hot sauce? The goal is to add a touch of sweetness with a little zing, so use your imagination—you probably have just the condiments waiting to be used.

Don't be afraid to make the basil aioli, home chef! Just zip up a few ingredients in a blender to create an aioli that sets these sandwiches apart. But you'll want to follow the instructions carefully or it won't emulsify properly. The first batch I made was a gloppy mess, and then I consulted my son-in-law, Stephen, who is a chemist. He gave me a lesson on the science of emulsification, which I have since forgotten, but at least I captured the basics in these instructions. Here's the good news: even if your batch fails to emulsify, it will still taste great, so go ahead and use it!

I haven't listed exact amounts here because you might eat seven of these sandwiches single-handedly, and I want to give you the freedom to do that.

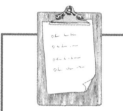

TO DO TONIGHT:
Start the Slow Cooker Caramelized Onions (page 227) so they can cook overnight for 12 hours in advance of tomorrow night's Caramelized Onion and Bacon Tart (page 225).

1. Either butter and grill the bread or simply toast it.

2. Schmear a thin layer (or thick—your choice!) of jam on the bread. Add layers of bacon (3 half slices in a row), lettuce or spinach, and shrimp.

3. Drizzle the aioli over the top and dive in (probably with a knife and fork)!

NOTE ON SHRIMP: You have a choice of a more expensive shortcut or a less expensive, more labor-intensive option. The shortcut is to go to a fish counter of a grocery store or fish market and buy boiled shrimp. This is an excellent option, since they generally have that yummy shrimp-boil seasoning. Pull them out of the fridge before you start prepping the sandwiches so they aren't ice-cold when they're added.

A less expensive option is pan-frying frozen shrimp, a quick and easy process. Place the frozen shrimp in a strainer and run water over them until they thaw. Peel the shrimp, then season with salt and pepper, or (even better) a little Cajun seasoning or your favorite seasoning. Heat a skillet with a bit of oil, then pan-fry the shrimp for 2 to 3 minutes, until they are opaque throughout.

BACON-TOMATO JAM

¾ cup chopped cooked
bacon (see page 217),
saved forward

1 pound tomatoes, cut
into medium dice

½ yellow onion, cut into
medium dice

¼ cup maple syrup

2½ tablespoons apple
cider vinegar

1 teaspoon table salt

¼ teaspoon ground black
pepper

1 teaspoon hot sauce of
your choice

1. Place the bacon, tomatoes, onion, maple syrup, vinegar, salt, pepper, and hot sauce in a medium saucepan over medium heat. Bring to a simmer and cook on low for 30 to 45 minutes, stirring occasionally. The resulting jam will have been cooked down until most of the liquid has evaporated.

2. Store the jam in the refrigerator for up to a week if you are a rule follower, perhaps longer if you like to play a little fast and loose.

BASIL AIOLI

1 cup mayonnaise

½ cup fresh basil leaves, cut into thin strips

2 garlic cloves

1 teaspoon lemon zest

¼ teaspoon table salt

1 tablespoon freshly squeezed lemon juice

1. In a blender or food processor, blend the mayonnaise and basil until the basil is well incorporated, scraping down the sides of the bowl frequently. Add the garlic, lemon zest, and salt and process a bit longer, until incorporated. Add the lemon juice slowly while the blender is running and blend until smooth.

2. Store the basil aioli in the fridge for up to 10 days.

SAVE IT FORWARD—BASIL AIOLI: You'll use the leftover Basil Aioli in Mediterranean Pasta Salad (page 223).

MEDITERRANEAN PASTA SALAD

1 tablespoon olive oil

1½ cups thin, 2-inch-long red bell pepper strips

1 cup 2-inch-long red or yellow onion slivers

2 garlic cloves, minced

¼ teaspoon table salt, plus more to taste

12 ounces penne or rotini pasta, cooked (see page 216), saved forward

1⅓ cups cherry tomatoes, halved and lightly salted

¼ to ½ cup pepperoni or Italian salami, sliced into thin strips

¼ cup olive tapenade, saved forward, or chopped olives

¼ cup finely chopped sun-dried tomatoes, saved forward

2 tablespoons drained capers (optional, if you have them)

½ cup Mediterranean Herb Feta Crumbles (such as Athenos brand) or regular feta with a bit of dried oregano

¼ cup grated Parmesan

½ cup Basil Aioli (page 222), saved forward, or see Note on page 224

This pasta salad is a delightful reincarnation of some of the ingredients you've used this week, so it's both time- and dollar-saving. If you're feeding picky eaters, adjust some of the ingredients to make them less bold: substitute milder cheeses (perhaps in cute little cubes), skip the capers, and chop the peppers and onions into smaller, less noticeable pieces. Picky eaters might be enchanted with chopped dill pickles as well. If you're feeding carnivores, add more pepperoni, even some leftover bacon (if they haven't already wiped it out); diced ham would likely thrill them too. Serve with Caramelized Onion and Bacon Tart (page 225).

1 tablespoon vinegar (red wine, white wine, or apple cider)

Freshly ground black pepper

Bread crumbs (see page 214), saved forward, or packaged crumbs (optional)

1. In a medium skillet, heat the olive oil over medium-high heat. Add the peppers and onions and sauté until they begin to get tender, 5 to 7 minutes. Add the garlic and salt and sauté until fragrant, about 30 seconds. Remove from the heat.

2. In a large microwave-safe bowl, splash a few drops of water over the pasta and heat for a couple of minutes, or until barely warm. Add the pepper and onion mixture, tomatoes, pepperoni, olive tapenade, sun-dried tomatoes, capers, feta, and Parmesan. Toss to combine. Add the Basil Aioli and vinegar and toss again. Taste and add a few grinds of pepper and salt, if needed.

3. If the pasta is too dry, add more Basil Aioli, if you have it, or a bit more olive oil and vinegar.

4. If you were super industrious earlier in the week and made bread crumbs, sprinkle them on top before serving, if you like.

NOTE ON BASIL AIOLI: You can sub bottled Italian dressing with slivers of fresh basil or a bit of dried basil for the Basil Aioli if need be.

CARAMELIZED ONION AND BACON TART

1 sheet frozen Pepperidge Farm puff pastry

1½ cups grated Gruyère or Swiss cheese (or cheese of your choice)

¼ cup Crème Fraîche (page 226; see Note)

5 slices cooked bacon (see page 217), saved forward, cut into ½-inch pieces

½ cup Slow Cooker Caramelized Onions (page 227)

Okay, so this might seem complicated, but let me walk you through it before you turn the page! There are two ingredients that require a day or two of prep in advance—Slow Cooker Caramelized Onions and Crème Fraîche—but they take about 5 minutes of effort (and see the Note for other crème fraîche options). You likely have some precooked bacon in the fridge, and the puff pastry is a prepared item from the freezer aisle, so it's just matter of assembling components. The end product is incredible, even guest-worthy—give it a whirl!

1. Prchcat the oven to 400°F.

2. Thirty minutes before you assemble the tart, remove the puff pastry from the freezer. Don't take it out much earlier because it won't unroll easily. After thawing, unroll the puff pastry on a sheet pan and prick the pastry sheet with a fork every few inches. If it isn't unrolling easily, throw it back into the freezer for a bit.

3. In a small bowl, mix the cheese and crème fraîche, then schmear it all over the puff pastry sheet, leaving a 1-inch border around the entire rectangle. Distribute the bacon and caramelized onions evenly over the cheese mixture.

4. Bake for 15 to 20 minutes, until the pastry is golden brown. Cut into rectangles for serving.

NOTE ON CRÈME FRAÎCHE: Sour cream or Greek yogurt would be a good substitution for crème fraîche, though a little more tart. City grocery stores sometimes sell packaged crème fraîche near the sour cream, though it is pricier than the homemade version.

CRÈME FRAÎCHE

1 cup heavy whipping
cream

3 tablespoons buttermilk

Crème fraîche is a thick, tangy, delightful cream, akin to sour cream but less tart. It will last about two weeks in the fridge, so if you're cooking Week 14, the Veggie-Forward, Fall-Winter Edition menu (page 229) next, you'll devour it with a couple of dishes that week. You may want to double the recipe!

1. Place the cream and buttermilk in a small container and stir. Cover with a cheesecloth or thin cotton tea towel and secure with a rubber band.

2. Let the container sit out in a warm place in the house for 24 hours, or even a bit longer is fine.

3. Remove the cheesecloth, stir, and marvel at how the mixture has thickened. To thicken even further, place the container in the refrigerator for another 24 hours and stir again.

SLOW COOKER CARAMELIZED ONIONS

5 yellow onions, cut lengthwise into ¼-inch-thick slices

5 tablespoons butter, melted

1 teaspoon table salt

Have you ever made caramelized onions on the stove? Though delicious, they are a major hassle, with forty-five minutes of near-constant stirring, plus your house smells like a diner for a week. I wish I knew the genius who came up with this slow cooker method so I could send her a patty melt as an expression of my love. When I make this recipe, I often double it, because you'll also use the onions in a couple recipes in Week 14, the Veggie-Forward Fall-Winter Edition menu (page 229), if you're cooking that next.

This slow cooker version is virtually hands-off, though it does take twelve hours of cooking. Warning: I would put the slow cooker in your garage or somewhere outside the house. Caramelized onions kick up quite an aroma, but at least you can move the slow cooker outside your living area.

1. Place the onions in the crock of a slow cooker, then drizzle with the butter and salt and toss to combine. Cook on low for 12 hours. If at some point you can stir the onions, do so, but no need to set the alarm for two a.m. if you're cooking them overnight.

2. The onions will last in the refrigerator for 10 days, but I usually just package them in 1-cup servings and freeze for later use.

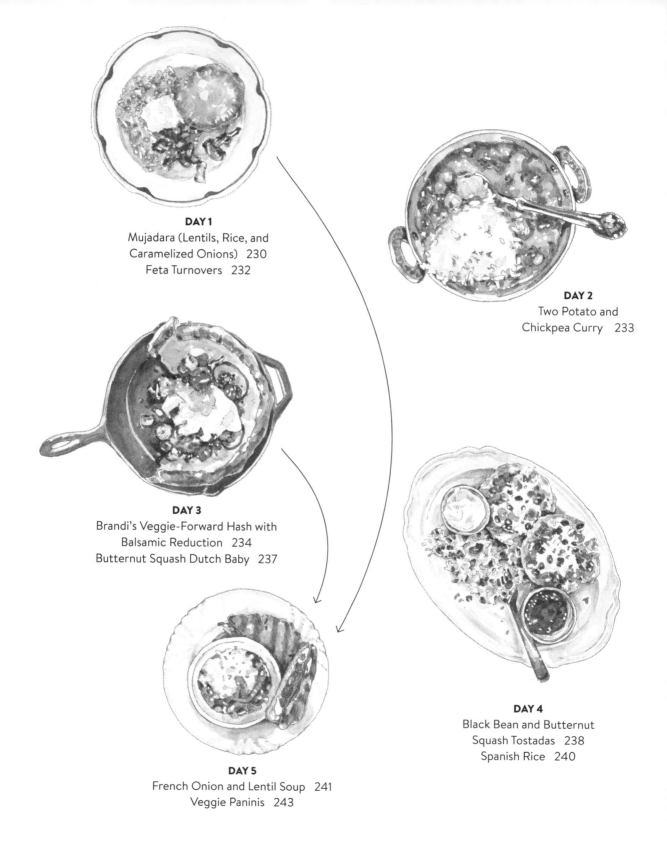

DAY 1
Mujadara (Lentils, Rice, and
Caramelized Onions) 230
Feta Turnovers 232

DAY 2
Two Potato and
Chickpea Curry 233

DAY 3
Brandi's Veggie-Forward Hash with
Balsamic Reduction 234
Butternut Squash Dutch Baby 237

DAY 4
Black Bean and Butternut
Squash Tostadas 238
Spanish Rice 240

DAY 5
French Onion and Lentil Soup 241
Veggie Paninis 243

Veggie-Forward Week, Fall-Winter Edition

Consider making these meal components on the weekend to make your life a breeze during the coming week. A few of this week's recipes use cooked butternut squash and sweet potatoes, so I decided to throw them in a slow cooker and see what would happen. It worked like a charm! I didn't use any water; I just washed them, threw them in the crock, and set the temp to low. This method works well if you are going to be around the house because the vegetables cook at different rates, so they need to be removed from the crock at separate times. If this method is too loosey-goosey for you, I understand! Just cook them in your usual way. But it's smart to cook them in advance to expedite this week's meals.

I tried russet potatoes in the slow cooker as well but they took forever, so go with your oven for those. And for the rice, just use your usual method.

- Caramelized onions: You may have some caramelized onions left over if you cooked Week 13's Mediterranean Week, but if not, see page 227 for my easy Slow Cooker Caramelized Onions, which can be cooking by night while your squash and potatoes cook by day.
- 1 butternut squash: Cook in the slow cooker on low for about 3 to 4 hours, depending on the size, flipping over at 1½ hours, if you can. Then peel (or not!) and stash in the fridge.
- 3 medium sweet potatoes (3 pounds): Cook in the slow cooker on low for approximately 4 hours, depending on the size, then peel (or not!) and stash in the fridge.
- 4 medium russet potatoes (3 pounds): Bake at 375°F for 1 to 1½ hours, then peel (or not!) and stash in the fridge. Bonus tip: I pierce mine with a fork a few times before I place them in the oven to prevent a messy potato explosion.
- White rice: Cook a quantity suitable as a side dish for Two Potato and Chickpea Curry (page 233) plus 2 to 4 additional cups for Spanish Rice (page 240).

NOTE ON BUTTERNUT SQUASH: *Two of this week's recipes call for cooked butternut squash, but no worries if you didn't complete the weekend prep above. Packaged butternut squash cubes are easily found in the freezer and refrigerated produce sections. Just follow the microwave cooking instructions on the package.*

MUJADARA (LENTILS, RICE, AND CARAMELIZED ONIONS)

8 cups (2 quarts) Overnight Chicken broth (page 268) or other chicken broth

5 garlic cloves, minced

2 bay leaves

2 teaspoons table salt

2 teaspoons freshly ground black pepper

2 cups uncooked white rice

2 cups brown or green lentils, rinsed

1 teaspoon olive oil

¼ teaspoon ground cumin

¾ cup Slow Cooker Caramelized Onions (page 227), saved forward

Plain Greek yogurt or Crème Fraîche (page 226)

Hot sauce, for serving (optional)

Who knew that humble lentils and rice could be so flavorful? Though I'm not Middle Eastern, I'm embracing the region's comfort food as my own! This recipe makes a large batch, because you'll be saving forward the leftovers for French Onion and Lentil Soup (page 241) later in the week. Plus, the leftovers make a delightful lunch! Serve with Feta Turnovers (page 232).

**LUNCH BITS
AND BOBS:**
*Mujadara reheats
well as is, and you
can also trick it up a
bit by adding diced
cooked butternut
squash or sweet
potatoes from your
weekend prep.*

1. In a large pot, combine the chicken broth, 2 cups of water, the garlic, bay leaves, salt, and pepper. Bring the mixture to a boil over medium-high heat and add the rice and lentils. Cover the pot, reduce the heat to medium-low, and simmer until the liquid is absorbed and the rice and lentils are tender, approximately 20 minutes. Discard the bay leaves.

2. Meanwhile, in a small skillet over medium heat, heat the olive oil. Add the cumin and stir until fragrant. Add the caramelized onions and cook for 3 to 5 minutes, until warm and even more aromatic.

3. Serve the lentils and rice with a dollop of yogurt or crème fraîche and top with a spoonful of caramelized onions. A dash of hot sauce is essential for me, but skip it for a milder flavor.

SAVE IT FORWARD—LENTILS AND RICE: Reserve 3 cups of the lentils and rice for French Onion and Lentil Soup (page 241).

FETA TURNOVERS

1 can of biscuits with flaky layers

Mediterranean Herb Feta Crumbles (such as Athenos brand) or regular feta with a bit of dried oregano, 1 heaping tablespoon per biscuit

Cooking oil

I'm not going to pretend these turnovers are healthy—they're fried bread dough, after all. But they're a tasty little treat, and you can whip them up while the lentils and rice for the mujadara are cooking. These take me back to fifth grade and my very first cooking project: fried biscuit turnovers with jelly filling. My grown-up self has subbed feta for Welch's jelly because I'm fancy like that. But not so fancy that I won't use canned biscuits.

1. Open the can of biscuits and separate the individual biscuits. Split a biscuit into two halves and press them with your fingers to make them a bit thinner. Place a heaping tablespoon of feta in the middle of one half, then top it with the other half. Crimp all around the edges with a fork to seal the cheese in the middle. Repeat to make as many turnovers as you like.

2. Pour ½ inch of cooking oil into a heavy skillet and turn the heat to medium. Heat the oil to 350°F, or until a bit of pinched-off dough sizzles immediately when added.

3. Place the turnovers into the hot oil, leaving some space in the skillet between them. Depending on how many you are making and the size of your skillet, you may need to fry in batches. Fry for about 2 minutes per side, until golden brown. Remove from the skillet and place on a paper towel–lined plate to absorb the excess oil.

4. Serve warm or at room temperature.

TWO POTATO AND CHICKPEA CURRY

1 tablespoon olive oil

½ yellow onion, cut into medium dice

2 medium fresh tomatoes, cut into medium dice, or one 14.5-ounce can diced tomatoes, drained

2 garlic cloves, minced

1 teaspoon table salt, plus more to taste

1½ tablespoons garam masala

1 teaspoon curry powder

½ teaspoon ground cumin

⅛ teaspoon cayenne pepper

One 15-ounce can chickpeas, undrained

1 cooked sweet potato (see page 229), saved forward, peeled and cut into 1½-inch chunks

2 cooked russet potatoes (see page 229), saved forward, peeled and cut into 1-inch chunks

One 13.5-ounce can unsweetened coconut milk (I used full-fat, but I bet low-fat would work)

4 handfuls baby spinach

Juice from half a lime

Ground black pepper

Cooked rice (see page 229), saved forward, for serving

It was one of those rare occasions when I was at home by myself, which meant I got to tinker around with a vegetarian dish without the input of my carnivorous husband and children. When my tinkering was finished, I had created a dish that I happily ate for three days. I'm not generally a sweet potato fan, but I love them here, so be not afraid if you share my disdain for sweet potatoes.

1. In a large, deep skillet over medium heat, heat the olive oil. Add the onion and tomatoes and sauté for 3 to 5 minutes, until they start to soften. Add the garlic, salt, garam masala, curry powder, cumin, and cayenne and cook, stirring occasionally, for a couple of minutes until the spices become fragrant.

2. Add the undrained chickpeas, the two kinds of potatoes, and the coconut milk. Bring the mixture to a boil, then reduce the heat to low and let simmer for 5 minutes or so, covered, stirring occasionally. Stir in the spinach and let it cook for a couple of minutes until the spinach wilts. Add the lime juice, stir, and add salt and black pepper, if needed.

3. Serve over cooked rice.

BRANDI'S VEGGIE-FORWARD HASH with BALSAMIC REDUCTION

Butternut Squash Dutch
Baby (optional; page 237),
for serving

BALSAMIC REDUCTION

1 cup balsamic vinegar

1 tablespoon brown sugar

2 garlic cloves, peeled
and smashed

3 or 4 fresh thyme sprigs

HASH

3 ounces prosciutto,
diced

¼ cup olive oil

2 cooked medium sweet
potatoes (see page 229),
saved forward, peeled and
cut into 1-inch dice

2 cooked medium russet
potatoes (see page 229),
saved forward, peeled and
cut into 1-inch dice

2 teaspoons ground
cumin

1 teaspoon table salt

½ teaspoon freshly
ground black pepper

8 ounces Brussels sprouts,
trimmed and quartered

1 medium red onion, cut
into medium dice

8 ounces baby portobello
mushrooms, sliced

My friend and recipe tester, Brandi, created this sublime recipe. The scrumptious hash is served atop a Dutch baby, which is the mysterious marriage of a pancake and a popover. The hash's balsamic glaze is the pièce de résistance—don't skip it! It's easy to make, but you can also buy it in the store if you prefer.

Start the Dutch baby first if you are making it to serve with the hash—it's just a matter of whizzing up the batter in a blender and popping it in the oven for twenty-five minutes or so. Tackle the hash next, starting with the balsamic reduction, then prepping all the veggies so they're ready for some skillet magic. By the time the hash is finished, the glorious Dutch baby will be coming out of the oven, ready to serve as a platter for the hash.

Though I just touted the glorious Dutch baby, I want to assure you that you can skip it and still live a meaningful life; the hash is delightful on its own!

1. If you're making the Dutch baby, follow that recipe's directions and get it in the oven before you start working on the hash.

2. To make the balsamic reduction, in a small saucepan combine the balsamic vinegar, brown sugar, garlic, and thyme. Bring to a boil over medium-high heat, watching carefully so it doesn't boil over. Reduce the heat to medium and cook for 10 to 15 minutes, until reduced by half and the glaze is thick enough to coat the back of a spoon. Strain out the thyme sprigs and garlic and set the reduction aside to cool.

¼ cup vegetable broth (or sub chicken broth or water)

3 garlic cloves, minced

2 handfuls baby spinach

¼ cup grated Parmesan

¼ cup chopped fresh flat-leaf parsley

Fried or poached eggs, for serving (optional)

3. To make the hash, heat a 12-inch skillet (see Note on page 236) over medium heat and cook the prosciutto until browned and crispy. There is little fat on prosciutto, so stir often to prevent burning. Set aside on a paper towel–lined plate.

4. In the same skillet, heat the olive oil over medium-high heat. Add the sweet potatoes and russet potatoes and press them down lightly in the skillet. Cook for 5 minutes, undisturbed. Though you want to leave the potatoes undisturbed so that they develop a nice crust, after 3 minutes, gently lift up an edge to make sure they aren't burning, since skillets and stoves can vary. Don't be afraid to form a nice crust, but adjust the heat if the crust is getting too dark.

5. Flip the potatoes, lifting the browned bits off the bottom of the pan with a metal spatula. Sprinkle with the cumin, salt, and pepper. Add the Brussels sprouts and onion and toss with the potatoes. Turn the heat down to medium and cook for 5 to 8 minutes, stirring gently and occasionally, but leaving largely undisturbed except to check for burning. Cook until the veggies are tender and the potatoes have formed a browned exterior.

6. Add the mushrooms, broth or water, and garlic, stir to combine, and cook for 5 minutes more, or until the mushrooms are softened.

7. Turn off the heat and fold in the spinach. (The residual heat will cook the spinach down a bit.)

8. If you made the Dutch baby, cut it into serving-size pieces and add the hash on top. If you opted out of the Dutch baby, just divide the hash among plates. Drizzle with the balsamic reduction and sprinkle with the crispy prosciutto, Parmesan, and parsley. And a runny egg, if you like that sort of thing!

NOTE ON SKILLET: A well-seasoned cast-iron skillet is greatly preferable when cooking this recipe. If you don't have one, add a couple of additional tablespoons of oil and check frequently for burning.

SAVE IT FORWARD—HASH: Reserve ¼ cup per sandwich for Veggie Paninis (page 243).

SAVE IT FORWARD—BALSAMIC REDUCTION: Any leftovers will be a great addition to your Veggie Paninis!

BUTTERNUT SQUASH DUTCH BABY

¾ cup cooked and peeled butternut squash (see page 229), saved forward

½ cup all-purpose flour

¼ cup grated Parmesan

1 tablespoon sugar

2 teaspoons minced fresh thyme leaves

¾ teaspoon salt

½ teaspoon ground black pepper

4 large eggs, at room temperature

1 cup 2% milk

4 tablespoons (½ stick) butter, cubed

This Dutch baby is an absolute wonder—like a giant popover in a skillet! It puffs up, so you might want to gather the family and peer into the oven for this marvelous occurrence. It will deflate soon after it leaves the oven, but by then, you'll be happily devouring it.

1. Preheat the oven to 425°F. Place a 10-inch cast-iron skillet (or other heavy, ovenproof pan or skillet of similar size) in the oven immediately so that the pan has plenty of time to get very hot.

2. The butternut squash should be very soft. If it needs to be cooked a bit more, place it in a microwave-safe bowl with a little water and microwave, covered, for 3 to 4 minutes. Drain.

3. In a large bowl, whisk the flour, Parmesan, sugar, thyme, salt, and pepper. Place the eggs, milk, and squash in a blender and process until well blended. Add the flour mixture to the blender and pulse until combined.

4. Remove the skillet or pan from the oven, add the butter cubes, and place it back in the oven until the butter is melted. Remove the skillet from the oven and carefully tip it to coat with the melted butter.

5. Pour the batter into the hot skillet and bake for 25 to 30 minutes, until the Dutch baby is gloriously puffed and the sides are golden brown and crisp.

BLACK BEAN AND BUTTERNUT SQUASH TOSTADAS

3 cups ½-inch-diced cooked and peeled butternut squash (see page 229), saved forward

1 tablespoon olive oil

½ teaspoon chili powder

¼ teaspoon ground cumin

½ teaspoon table salt

¼ teaspoon ground black pepper

1 package tostadas, such as Mission brand Estilo Tostada Caseras (see Note)

One 10-ounce can enchilada sauce

¼ cup canned seasoned black beans, drained, per tostada (one 15-ounce can makes 6 tostadas)

2 tablespoons grated cheddar or pepper Jack cheese per tostada

Sour cream or Crème Fraîche (page 226), saved forward, for serving

Salsa, for serving

In case you have never noticed corn tostadas in your grocery store, you can find them either with the taco shells or on the Mexican food aisle. They are a flat, crunchy corn tortilla, packaged in a vertical stack. I suppose you could fry your own corn tortillas, but these are mighty handy and tasty! Serve with Spanish Rice (page 240).

1. Preheat the oven to 400°F and line a sheet pan with foil.

2. Place the cooked butternut squash on the sheet pan, drizzle it with the oil, and toss to coat well. Mix the chili powder, cumin, salt, and pepper in a small bowl, sprinkle the mixture over the butternut squash, and toss the squash again.

3. Spread the squash in a single layer on the pan and roast for 20 to 25 minutes or until browned. Once the squash is roasted, remove the foil with the squash from the sheet pan and set aside.

4. Place the tostadas on the sheet pan with a fresh sheet of foil. On top of each tostada, spread a layer of enchilada sauce, ¼ cup black beans, ½ cup roasted squash, and 2 tablespoons cheese.

5. Turn the oven temperature to broil and place the sheet pan of assembled tostadas on a top rack in the oven to melt the cheese. Watch them carefully!

NOTE ON TOSTADAS: The standard package of tostadas will likely have more tostadas than you will eat for one meal. They save indefinitely in the freezer, though—make your own save-it-forward creation with them!

SPANISH RICE

Since you cleverly cooked the rice in advance, this will come together quickly. The butter in this recipe is unexpected in Spanish rice, but it's wonderfully flavorful with the cumin. If you have a larger family, you may want to double this recipe.

2 tablespoons butter

1 teaspoon ground cumin

One 10-ounce can diced tomatoes and green chiles

Salt, to taste

2 cups cooked rice (see page 229), saved forward

Melt the butter in a large skillet over medium heat. Add the cumin and stir until fragrant, about 1 minute. Add the tomatoes and green chiles and salt and bring to a simmer for a couple of minutes to reduce the liquid a bit. Add the rice, stir to combine, and heat for a few minutes, until warmed.

FRENCH ONION AND LENTIL SOUP

This recipe came together with mysterious alchemy: I had some caramelized onions in the fridge, which prompted me to think of other uses, including French onion soup, of course. I also had Mujadara left over in the fridge, and I thought, why not add that to the soup? This soup has the delicious French onion flavors but with a hearty, stick-to-your-ribs quality of lentils and rice. Serve with Veggie Paninis (page 243).

3 cups Slow Cooker Caramelized Onions (page 227)

2 tablespoons flour

8 cups (2 quarts) beef broth

3 cups Mujadara lentils and rice (see page 230), saved forward

2 tablespoons Worcestershire sauce

1 tablespoon balsamic vinegar

2 bay leaves

2 fresh thyme sprigs or ½ teaspoon dried thyme leaves

1. In a large pot over medium-low heat, heat the caramelized onions. Add the flour, stir, and continue cooking for a couple of minutes, stirring constantly, until the flour is well incorporated.

2. Add the broth, lentils and rice, Worcestershire, balsamic vinegar, bay leaves, and thyme to the pot. Bring to a boil, lower the heat to a simmer, and cook for 10 to 15 minutes, until the soup is slightly thickened and the flavors are melded. Discard the bay leaves and any large thyme stems.

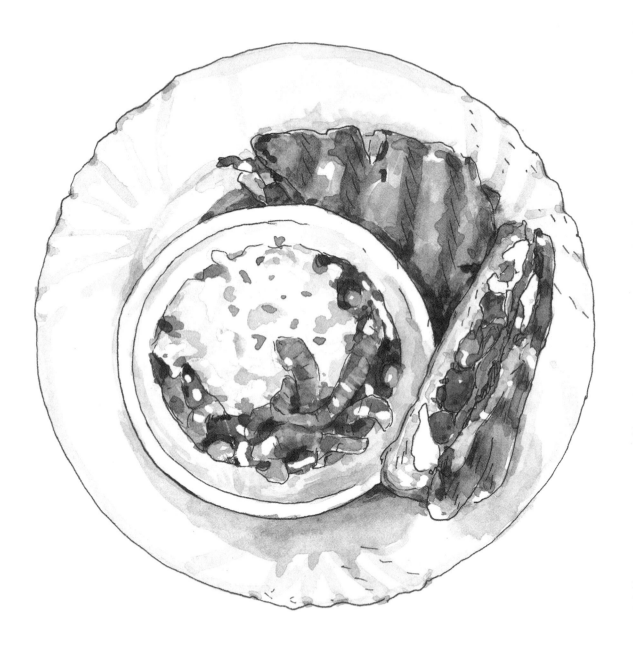

VEGGIE PANINIS

Brandi's Veggie-Forward Hash (page 234), saved forward, approximately ¼ cup per sandwich

Sturdy bread, such as ciabatta

Dijon mustard

Fresh mozzarella, thinly sliced

Black Forest ham, 1 or 2 slices per sandwich (optional)

Balsamic reduction, saved forward from Brandi's Veggie-Forward Hash (page 234)

Butter, softened

Day 3's Brandi's Veggie-Forward Hash is transformed here into delicious Veggie Paninis! This is my ideal combination of sandwich ingredients, but use your imagination to personalize it according to your taste.

1. Warm the hash in the microwave and roughly chop the veggies to make them a manageable size for a sandwich.

2. For each sandwich, layer the following on a piece of sturdy bread: a smear of Dijon, fresh mozzarella, ham, hash, a drizzle of balsamic reduction, and another layer of mozzarella (if you like a cheesy sandwich). Top it with another piece of bread, then butter the outside of the top and bottom of the sandwich.

3. Grill the sandwich in a hot panini maker until golden and crisp. If you don't have a panini maker, you can grill the sandwich in a skillet, laying another heavy skillet on top of the sandwich to press it together. Flip the sandwich to grill the other side.

4. Slice the sandwiches and serve.

DAY 1
Grilled Pork Loin and Tangy Potato
and Green Bean Salad   251

DAY 2
Chicken Quesadillas   252
Mexican Corn, Avocado,
and Black Bean Salad   254

DAY 3
Stuffed Peppers over Pasta
with the Simplest Tomato
Sauce   255

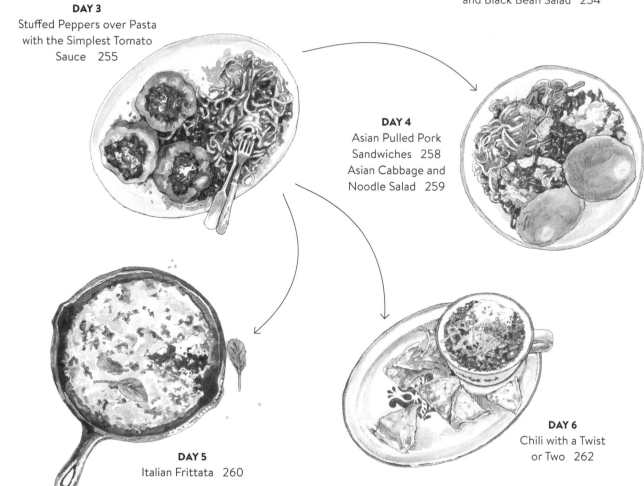

DAY 4
Asian Pulled Pork
Sandwiches   258
Asian Cabbage and
Noodle Salad   259

DAY 5
Italian Frittata   260

DAY 6
Chili with a Twist
or Two   262

WEEK 15
Mad Skills Week

This week's prep is a tad more advanced, but if you've cooked any of the prior weeks, I have full confidence in the mad skills you've developed. None of these meals is difficult to prepare; you just need to be a little organized—but hey, that's why you bought this book! I've done all the thinking for you, and you get to enjoy a week of delicious meals.

ADVANCE PREP

With a bit of work on Day 1, you'll have a refrigerator full of components to work with all week—*woohoo*! Turn the page for the life-saving details.

- 2 pounds of uncooked pork loin for Asian Pulled Pork Sandwiches (page 258)
- 2 pounds of cooked pork loin for Grilled Pork Loin (page 251)
- Grilled chicken for Chicken Quesadillas (page 252)
- Everyday Vinaigrette and blanched corn for Mexican Corn, Avocado, and Black Bean Salad (page 254)
- Blanched green beans and grilled new potatoes for Tangy Potato and Green Bean Salad (page 251)
- Additional veggies for Asian Cabbage and Noodle Salad (page 259) and possibly **Lunch Bits and Bobs**

A Save-It-Forward Extravaganza!

You're going to own this week, my friend! You'll spend a little time cooking, likely over the weekend, which will launch you into your week with a fridge full of components for later meals. Here's your game plan: Today, Day 1, you'll be grilling pork and chicken, using some of the same marinade ingredients for both, which streamlines the process. You'll devour the grilled pork tonight and save the chicken for Day 2's Mexican meal. Once you have the grill fired up, you'll grill some potatoes for tonight's salad.

Meanwhile, back inside the house, you'll blanch some veggies on the stove to be used in a variety of ways this week. Along with them, you'll be making a larger-than-usual batch of Everyday Vinaigrette: some for tonight and some to save forward.

Step 1: Early in the Day— Marinate the Meats and Make the Vinaigrette

The base marinade for the pork makes enough for one batch of pork or chicken. If you're cooking both the pork and chicken (of course you are, right?!), use the assembly line method to dump duplicate ingredients into two resealable bags or bowls. Then you'll add a few extra ingredients to the chicken marinade. This is also an excellent time to make a double batch of this week's Everyday Vinaigrette (page 269) since it uses some of the same ingredients.

MARINATE THE PORK

Though you are buying a 4-pound pork loin, aka half loin, only half of it will be used in tonight's Grilled Pork Loin (page 251); half will be saved forward, so pop it in a zip-top bag for use later in the week.

BASE MARINADE
⅓ cup olive oil
1 teaspoon garlic powder
1 teaspoon dried oregano
1 teaspoon paprika
1 teaspoon table salt

One 4-pound pork loin
(2 pounds cut into 1-inch-thick slices; 2 pounds reserved as a **SAVE-IT-FORWARD** item)

Place the base marinade ingredients in a resealable bag or bowl and whisk or smush (that's a culinary term) them together. Add the pork loin slices and coat them with the marinade. Refrigerate for at least 3 hours if you have the time, but you can marinate for less time or even overnight.

MARINATE THE CHICKEN

I admit that 2 pounds of grilled chicken thighs is a lot just for tomorrow's Chicken Quesadillas (page 252), but I like to make extra quesadillas for **Lunch Bits and Bobs**, or just to have extra grilled chicken on hand for salads and such. Feel free to use only 1 pound if you don't want leftovers. Chicken breasts are fine, too; I just think thighs stay juicier when you grill them.

MARINADE

⅓ cup olive oil
1 teaspoon garlic powder
1 teaspoon dried oregano
1 teaspoon paprika
1 teaspoon table salt
1 teaspoon onion powder
1 teaspoon ground cumin
1 teaspoon chili powder

¼ cup juice from a jar of pickled jalapeños (optional; will add flavor, not heat)
Juice of 1 small lemon (about 2 tablespoons)

2 pounds boneless chicken thighs (a **SAVE-IT-FORWARD** item)

1. Place the marinade ingredients in a resealable bag or bowl and mix to combine. Add the chicken, coating it with the marinade.
2. Refrigerate for at least 3 hours if you have the time, but you can marinate for less time or even overnight.

MAKE THE EVERYDAY VINAIGRETTE

Double the recipe for Everyday Vinaigrette (page 269) and skip the optional herbs.

Step 2: Close to Dinnertime—
Fire Up the Grill for Potato Packets, Pork, and Chicken

Now you'll grill the Potato Packets and the pork and chicken!

GRILL THE POTATO PACKETS

This quantity of potatoes is the amount for tonight's salad, but my teenage boys always want more than this to eat as a stand-alone potato dish. So, if your household is like mine, you'll want to increase your quantity!

1 pound small red potatoes, cut into halves
2 tablespoons olive oil
½ teaspoon garlic powder

¾ teaspoon seasoned salt
Ground black pepper, to taste

1. Make a foil packet by placing the potatoes on the center of a sheet of foil. (Make 2 packets if you increase your potato quantity.) Add the olive oil and seasonings and toss to coat. Place another sheet of foil on top and crimp the edges to seal. Pssst . . . here's an old Boy Scout trick: pop an ice cube or two into the packet(s) before closing it up to add moisture!
2. Heat the grill to medium heat, set the potato packet(s) on the grill, and close the lid. Cook for 10 minutes, then check for doneness. Flip the packet(s) to cook on the other side, and you will likely cook for another 10 minutes or more, depending on the heat of the grill. The potatoes will be tender when done (test with a skewer).

SKETCHY AND PATHETIC MEAT GRILLING INSTRUCTIONS

So, here's my disclaimer. I'm not a grillmeister, and everyone's grill is different. But here's what I did: I threw the marinated pork and chicken on the grill with the potatoes at medium heat, closed the lid, and walked away. I went to the kitchen and fiddled around with veggie prep. I'd say about 7 minutes or so later I went back out to the grill. The meat released from the grill easily, and I could see some magical grill marks, so I flipped it.

I went back into the kitchen, fiddled around for about 7 minutes more and went back outside with my meat thermometer. Both the pork and the chicken registered 165°F, which is safe to eat (the new pork guidelines say that 160°F is safe).

To sum it up, the pork and chicken need about 15 minutes of total cooking time, but you should be the judge of your own grill situation.

Step 3: Meanwhile, Back in the Kitchen— Veggie and Salad Prep

While the meat is grilling, hop back inside to blanch some veggies to save forward and make a quick salad for tonight!

If you've never blanched your veggies for a salad, try it just one time, and then we can chat about the merits when I meet you in person. The process is so quick, and your overly chewy veggies will have the perfect texture, and the flavor will become sweeter. You'll be blanching green beans for tonight's Tangy Potato and Green Bean Salad (page 251), but I'd also throw in some broccoli florets or asparagus to save forward for the Asian Cabbage and Noodle Salad (page 259).

If you want some **Lunch Bits and Bobs**, you can also blanch more veggies to add to salads throughout the week. Remember, you'll likely have some extra grilled chicken that you can put in lunch salads too!

BLANCH THE VEGGIES

Table salt
1 pound green beans, ends cut or snapped off
3 ears corn (a **SAVE-IT-FORWARD** item)

1 cup (or more for lunches!) additional veggies—broccoli, asparagus, and so on—cut into salad-size pieces (a **SAVE-IT-FORWARD** item)

1. Fill a large pot two-thirds full of water and add 1 tablespoon of salt. Prepare a large bowl of ice water and set aside.

2. Bring the water to a gentle boil over medium-high heat. Add the veggies, starting with the green beans; you'll blanch only one kind at a time. When they become bright in color, take one out and test to see if it is crisp but tender. When the veggies are blanched to your liking, scoop them out with a slotted spoon, small strainer, or tongs and transfer them to the bowl of ice water to stop the cooking.

When the veggies have cooled, remove them to drain on a kitchen towel. Repeat to blanch the rest of the veggies, still one kind at a time.

TIMING NOTE: Broccoli, asparagus, and green beans take 3 to 4 minutes to cook, depending on size; check them at 3 minutes, or even earlier if they are small. Corn takes about 4 minutes to cook.

SAVE IT FORWARD—CORN: If you're feeling super efficient, you can cut the corn off the cob, so it is already prepped for tomorrow's Mexican Corn, Avocado, and Black Bean Salad (page 254).

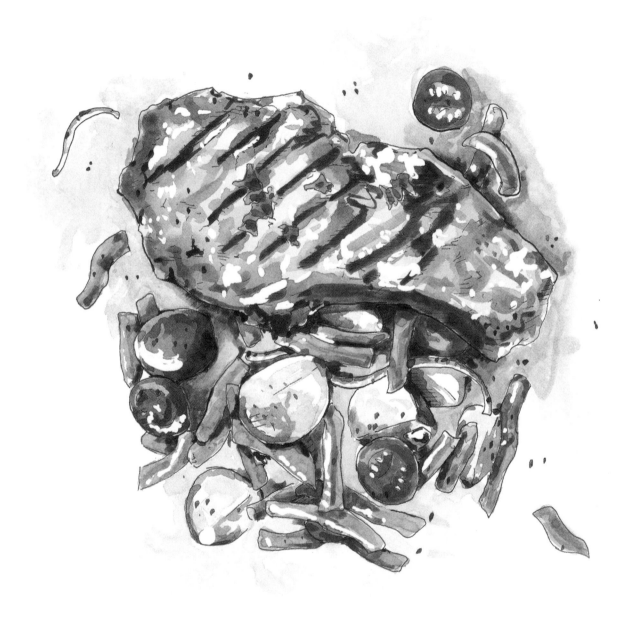

GRILLED PORK LOIN AND TANGY POTATO AND GREEN BEAN SALAD

1 pound fresh green beans, blanched (follow instructions for veggies on page 249) and cut into bite-size pieces

1 pound new potatoes, grilled (follow instructions for potato packets on page 248) and cut into quarters

1 cup cherry tomatoes, halved

¼ cup thinly sliced yellow onion

⅓ cup Everyday Vinaigrette (page 269)

2 pounds grilled pork loin (follow instructions on page 248), saved forward

This salad saves well, so hopefully you'll have some leftovers. It's particularly delicious with the frittata later in the week— if you can keep yourself out of it until then!

In a large bowl, combine the green beans, potatoes, tomatoes, and onion. Add the vinaigrette and gently toss to combine. Serve with the grilled pork loin.

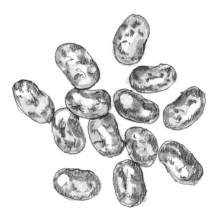

CHICKEN QUESADILLAS

½ cup mayonnaise

2 tablespoons finely chopped pickled jalapeños plus 2 tablespoons juice from the jar

Flour or corn tortillas, 2 per quesadilla, size of your choice

Shredded cheddar or pepper Jack cheese

Grilled chicken (see page 248), saved forward, cut into strips

Sour cream, salsa, pico de gallo, and/or guacamole, for garnish (optional)

Since the accompanying Mexican Corn, Avocado, and Black Bean Salad (page 254) is a tad fancy, I'm keeping the quesadillas simple, though I'm adding a jalapeño mayo to make them a little more special. If you want to keep them super simple, you can make these with just your save-it-forward grilled chicken and some cheese. You can't mess these up! If you cooked two pounds of chicken yesterday, you can also make extra quesadillas to stash in the freezer or eat for lunch (or just save the chicken for salads).

1. Preheat the oven to the lowest setting and place a sheet pan on the middle rack for keeping the quesadillas warm.

2. In a large bowl, combine the mayo, jalapeños, and juice. Spread a thin layer of the mayo mixture on one of the tortillas per quesadilla for those who want the heat.

3. Heat a large nonstick skillet over medium-high heat. Add a tortilla, sprinkle on a thin layer of cheese, add some of the grilled chicken, and sprinkle with more cheese. Top with a second tortilla and cook for 2 minutes, until golden, then flip and cook on the other side until golden and the cheese is melted.

4. Place the cooked quesadilla on the sheet pan in the warm oven while you cook the remaining quesadillas.

5. Slice the quesadillas into wedges for serving and top with your favorite garnishes. Sour cream and salsa are nonnegotiable at our house!

MEXICAN CORN, AVOCADO, AND BLACK BEAN SALAD

Kernels from 3 blanched ears corn (see page 249), saved forward (2 cups canned or frozen corn works, too!)

One 15-ounce can black beans, drained

½ small red onion, cut into small dice

½ cup roughly chopped fresh cilantro

20 cherry tomatoes, halved

Juice from 1 lime (about 2 tablespoons)

½ teaspoon ground cumin

Pinch of cayenne pepper, if you like heat (optional)

⅓ cup Everyday Vinaigrette (page 269), saved forward

1 avocado

Table salt and ground black pepper

This salad is a classic marriage of flavors, and if you can restrain yourself tonight, you'll enjoy the leftovers (see the **Lunch Bits and Bobs** *idea at the bottom of this page)!*

1. In a large bowl, combine the corn, black beans, onion, cilantro, and tomatoes.

2. Add the lime juice, cumin, and cayenne to the vinaigrette. Shake to combine, then dress the salad.

3. Pit and peel the avocado and cut it into ½-inch dice. Add the avocado right before serving. Taste the salad and add salt and pepper to taste.

LUNCH BITS AND BOBS: *If you have any leftover Grilled Chicken and Mexican Corn, Avocado, and Black Bean Salad, all you need is some crispy romaine lettuce to make a restaurant-quality salad. In your lunch bag, bring a small container of Everyday Vinaigrette to freshen the salad right before eating. You'll be the envy of the break room!*

STUFFED PEPPERS OVER PASTA WITH THE SIMPLEST TOMATO SAUCE

Three 14½-ounce cans whole San Marzano tomatoes

8 tablespoons (1 stick) butter

1½ small yellow onions, cut into three halves

Table salt and ground black pepper

6 bell peppers—red is prettiest, in my opinion!

1 pound spaghetti (a **SAVE-IT-FORWARD** item)

2½ pounds ground turkey or beef (a **SAVE-IT-FORWARD** item)

1 pound Italian sausage

1½ cups frozen riced cauliflower

8 ounces (2 cups) shredded mozzarella

Fasten your seat belts, friends—you're going to finish this meal with components for three future meals! Extra filling from the peppers will become a frittata, extra ground turkey and riced cauliflower will go into chili, and leftover spaghetti will be transformed into an Asian noodle salad.

Credit goes to Marcella Hazan, the famous Italian cook and writer, for her simple and ingenious three-ingredient tomato sauce, though I added salt and pepper, which technically makes it a five-ingredient sauce, but who's counting, right?

1. Preheat the oven to 350°F.

2. Fill a Dutch oven or large pot with water and bring to a slow boil.

3. While the water is coming to a boil, make the tomato sauce: In a medium saucepan over medium heat, combine the tomatoes, butter, and onions and cook until just starting to simmer and bubble. Bring to a low simmer and cook until the rest of the meal is ready, about 45 minutes, periodically smashing the tomatoes against the pan's side to break them down. Add salt and pepper to taste as the sauce cooks.

4. Remove the onion halves and set them aside; chop a single onion half for the stuffed pepper mixture and discard the others.

5. To prepare the peppers, rinse them, cut off the tops (save them—see Save It Forward—Red Pepper Tops on page 256!), and remove the ribs and seeds. Submerge the whole peppers

**SAVE IT FORWARD—
COOKED MEAT
MIXTURE:** Reserve
1½ cups of the cooked
meat mixture and
refrigerate it for use
in Italian Frittata
(page 260).

**SAVE IT FORWARD—
SPAGHETTI:** Save
2 cups of cooked
spaghetti for Asian
Cabbage and Noodle
Salad (page 259).

**SAVE IT FORWARD—
RED PEPPER TOPS:**
Cut the tops into a
medium dice and
reserve ⅓ cup to add
to Italian Frittata
(page 260). Any
additional peppers can
be added to the chili
meat prep (see **To Do
Tonight** on page 257).

in the slowly boiling water; the temperature will reduce to a simmer. Bring the water back to a boil, then turn down to a simmer and cook the peppers for 3 minutes, or until slightly softened. Using tongs or a small strainer with a handle, remove the peppers to a large bowl and drop an ice cube or two into each one to stop the cooking process. (Don't drain the pot of water; you'll need it for the spaghetti.) When the peppers are cool, drain them again and set aside.

6. To make the filling for the peppers, in a large skillet, combine 1 pound of the ground turkey or beef and the Italian sausage. Cook over medium heat, breaking up the meat with a spatula, until no longer pink, about 5 minutes. Drain the fat and return the meat to the skillet. (You'll be cooking the remaining 1½ pounds of turkey or beef shortly; see **To Do Tonight** on page 257!)

7. Add ½ cup of the cooked tomato sauce, the chopped cooked onion, the riced cauliflower, and ½ cup of the mozzarella to the meat mixture in the skillet and stir to combine. Cook until the mixture is bubbly. Taste and adjust the seasonings as desired.

8. To assemble, pour a 1-inch layer of the tomato sauce into a 9 x 13-inch baking dish. Sprinkle 1 cup of the meat mixture over the sauce.

9. Stuff ¾ cup of the meat mixture into each pepper, then top with a sprinkling of mozzarella. Place the stuffed peppers upright in the baking dish as you go. If you have any additional meat mixture left, you can add this to the tomato sauce in the baking dish.

10. Bake for 20 minutes, until the sauce is bubbly and the mozzarella is melted.

11. Meanwhile, cook the spaghetti in the pot of simmering water according to the package directions.

12. To serve, make a bed of pasta on each plate and ladle the tomato and meat sauce over it. Place a stuffed pepper artistically on the pasta, or just plunk it down in the middle like I did.

TO DO TONIGHT: *Before you wash the skillet, while the peppers are in the oven, cook the remaining 1½ pounds of turkey or beef for Chili with a Twist or Two (page 262). Add any remaining diced red pepper tops to the skillet with the meat. Cook on medium heat, breaking the meat up as it cooks. When the meat is no longer pink, drain the fat, then refrigerate the meat for effortless chili prep later in the week. Congratulate yourself on your efficiency!*

ASIAN PULLED PORK SANDWICHES

In our part of the world here in Oklahoma, "pulled pork" nearly always means barbecue, which bores me a tad. So I came up with an Asian version, complete with a lovely sauce for drizzling. Serve with Asian Cabbage and Noodle Salad (page 259).

2 pounds uncooked pork loin (see page 246), saved forward

2 tablespoons sesame oil

1 tablespoon ground ginger

2 tablespoons minced garlic

½ teaspoon table salt

½ teaspoon ground black pepper

½ cup rice wine vinegar or other vinegar

¼ cup soy sauce

2 tablespoons ketchup

1 to 2 tablespoons sriracha, to taste

¼ cup lightly packed brown sugar

1 tablespoon cornstarch

Hamburger or slider rolls, for serving

1. Trim the pork loin of any excess fat, though leaving a thin layer is fine. Make a paste of the sesame oil, ginger, garlic, salt, and pepper and rub all over the pork loin. Combine the vinegar, soy sauce, ketchup, sriracha, brown sugar, and ½ cup of water in a slow cooker and stir to combine. Add the pork loin and cook on low for 6 to 8 hours or on high for 4 to 6 hours, until the meat shreds easily with two forks.

2. Remove the pork to a cutting board. Let it cool slightly, then shred into bite-size pieces.

3. Pour all but 1 cup of the liquid from the slow cooker into a small saucepan and keep it warm on the stove. Return the meat to the slow cooker, stir it with the liquid remaining in the cooker, and set the cooker to warm.

4. To make the sauce, whisk the cornstarch and 1 tablespoon of water in a small bowl. Add the slurry to the sauce on the stove, bring to a boil, then lower the heat to a simmer and cook for 1 minute, until thickened, stirring constantly.

5. Serve the meat over warmed rolls and drizzle with the sauce.

ASIAN CABBAGE AND NOODLE SALAD

If you want to make this salad gluten-free or low-carb, just skip the spaghetti and add more cabbage. It's also great as a base for Asian Pulled Pork Sandwiches (page 258) if you want to skip the bun; you may want to double the salad recipe in that case.

½ small head Savoy cabbage (see Note), cut into thin shreds across the grain

2 cups cooked spaghetti (see page 256), saved forward, cut into bite-size pieces

1 cup fresh cilantro leaves, roughly chopped

1 cup chopped veggie of your choice (see page 249), saved forward

2 green onions, thinly sliced, or ¼ cup thinly sliced yellow or white onion

3 tablespoons sesame oil

2 tablespoons soy sauce

1 tablespoon freshly squeezed lime juice

1 tablespoon minced garlic

½ teaspoon sugar

½ teaspoon table salt, plus more to taste

¼ teaspoon ground black pepper, plus more to taste

1. In a large skillet over medium-high heat, combine the cabbage with ½ cup of water. Cook on medium-high heat until it turns bright green, about 4 minutes, stirring often. Drain off the excess water and add the spaghetti. Stir until warmed.

2. Place the cabbage and noodle mixture in a serving bowl and top it with the cilantro, chopped veggie, and green onions.

3. Whisk the sesame oil, soy sauce, lime juice, garlic, sugar, salt, and pepper in a medium bowl. Taste and adjust the seasonings. Pour the sauce over the vegetable and noodle mixture, stir to combine, and serve warm (or any temp is good!).

NOTE ON CABBAGE: I used Savoy cabbage, because it's frilly and pretty. If you want to be over the top, exchange some of the Savoy cabbage for purple cabbage for a lovely bit of color.

ITALIAN FRITTATA

2 tablespoons olive oil (or just enough to coat the pan)

⅓ cup finely chopped yellow onion

⅓ cup roughly chopped red bell pepper (see page 256), saved forward

1 generous handful baby spinach, stems removed

1½ cups cooked meat mixture (see page 256), saved forward

6 eggs, whisked with 2 tablespoons water

4 ounces fresh mozzarella, sliced thin

1 cup grated cheese of your choice (I use cheddar and Parmesan), plus more for serving if desired

Are frittatas part of your regular rotation? If not, you may become a believer after trying this one! It's unbelievably easy and quick to throw together, particularly when some of the components are saved forward from previous meals. Serve with buttered bread and any leftover salads you might have from earlier in the week, or heck, just eat half the frittata—it's healthy!

1. Preheat the broiler and set a rack in the center position.

2. Heat a 10-inch ovenproof (essential!) skillet over medium-high heat, add the olive oil, and heat until a piece of onion sizzles when it hits the pan. Add the onion and bell pepper and sauté until tender, about 5 to 7 minutes. Turn the heat to medium-low. Evenly distribute the spinach and meat mixture around the pan, cook for a couple of minutes, then pour in the eggs to distribute evenly. Sprinkle with the cheeses (they must be added last) and cook undisturbed until the eggs start to set, about 4 minutes. With a spatula, lift an edge of the frittata and make sure it looks golden brown on the bottom.

3. Set the pan in the broiler and broil until the cheese is melted and the eggs are completely set.

4. Cut into wedges and serve warm (or cooled—a frittata is good at any temperature!).

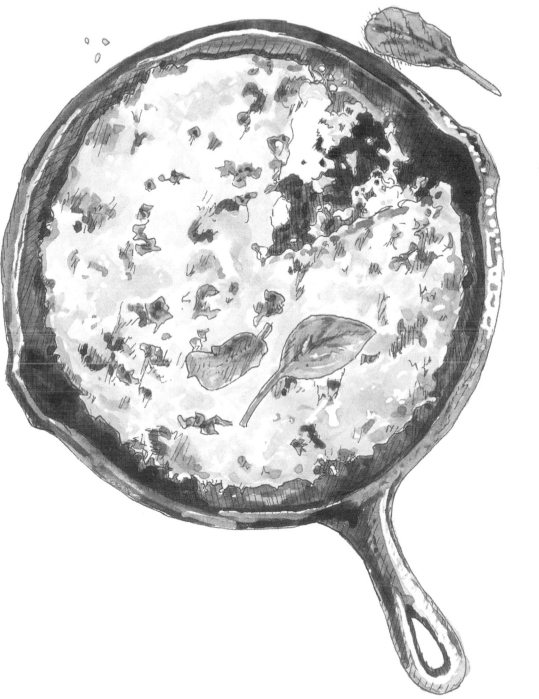

CHILI WITH A TWIST OR TWO

1½ pounds chili meat (see page 257), saved forward

½ onion, chopped

One 15-ounce can pinto beans, half the liquid drained

One 15-ounce can white beans, half the liquid drained

One 15-ounce can black beans, half the liquid drained

One 15-ounce can kidney beans, half the liquid drained

One 15-ounce can Ranch Style (or other chili-flavored) beans, undrained

3 cups medium diced zucchini

1½ cups frozen riced cauliflower

One 32-ounce carton tomato soup or tomato and red pepper soup (see Note on page 263)

1 teaspoon ground cumin

1 teaspoon garlic powder

1 teaspoon onion powder

1 tablespoon chili powder

A pinch or two of cayenne pepper

The men in my household are super picky about their chili. Well, not super picky, because those freaks also like canned chili. But they are resolute that chili should be made with beef. So, when I first made chili from turkey, I was expecting them to revolt and get pizza, and I'd have some fantastic lunch leftovers. To my surprise, they loved it—no leftovers, dang it. Even more surprising? They didn't even complain about the zucchini! And I totally tricked them with the cauliflower—they didn't even notice it. Heh heh.

I generally try to avoid processed foods, but I make an exception with this recipe, which includes packaged tomato soup. I highly recommend using it in chili; it adds a tomatoey creaminess that is so good. I recommend the organic tomato soup that comes in cartons and includes milk.

1. In the crock of a slow cooker add the meat, onions, beans, zucchini, cauliflower, tomato soup, cumin, garlic powder, onion powder, chili powder, cayenne pepper, salt, and black pepper. Cook on high for 4 to 5 hours or low for 6 to 8 hours. (Other options: Simmer on the stove for 1 hour or so or cook in an Instant Pot for 7 minutes on high pressure and do a quick release.) Taste and adjust the seasonings.

2. This chili is best served with all the chili fixins: corn chips or tortilla chips, sour cream, and/or grated cheese.

1 teaspoon table salt, plus more to taste

1 teaspoon ground black pepper, plus more to taste

Optional for serving: corn chips or tortilla chips, sour cream, grated cheese, cilantro

NOTE ON TOMATO SOUP: If you can't find tomato soup in a carton, sub a 28-ounce can of crushed tomatoes or two cans of the old faithful red-and-white-label condensed tomato soup made with 2 soup cans' worth of milk.

Essentials and Extras

This is an odd assortment of a few things that I couldn't resist sharing with you. Many of these recipes, such as those made in a slow cooker, have become essential in my arsenal of easy, go-to dinners. The sauces and other items are extras just for fun. But shouldn't we have fun extras in our meals? Maybe they're all essential—you be the judge!

SKILLET CORNBREAD

1¼ cups cornmeal

¾ cup all-purpose flour (or cup-for-cup gluten-free flour)

¼ cup granulated sugar

1 teaspoon kosher salt

2 teaspoons baking powder

½ teaspoon baking soda

⅓ cup whole milk

1 cup buttermilk

2 eggs, lightly whisked

8 tablespoons (1 stick) unsalted butter, melted, plus 1 tablespoon

My husband is a gluten-free guy, and I generally judge gluten-free bread products as subpar, but not this cornbread! The recipe calls for regular all-purpose flour for those who can tolerate it, but I sub the gluten-free flour that measures the same.

1. Preheat the oven to 425°F and place a 9-inch cast-iron skillet inside to heat while making the batter.

2. In a large bowl, whisk the cornmeal, flour, sugar, salt, baking powder, and baking soda. Add the milk and buttermilk and stir to combine. Add the eggs and stir to combine. Whisk in the melted butter.

3. Carefully remove the hot skillet from the oven. Reduce the oven temperature to 375°F. Add the remaining tablespoon of butter and swirl it around the pan to melt. Pour the batter evenly into the skillet and place it in the center of the oven. Bake until the center is firm and a cake tester or toothpick inserted into the center comes out clean, 20 to 25 minutes.

4. Let cool for 10 to 15 minutes before serving.

EVERYDAY SLOW COOKER CHICKEN

1 whole chicken,
approximately 5 to
6 pounds

2 teaspoons paprika

2 teaspoons garlic powder

1 teaspoon onion powder

1 teaspoon table salt

½ teaspoon ground black
pepper

Cooking spray

2 carrots, cut into chunks

½ onion, peeled and cut
into wedges

This is not a lovely, browned chicken that you'll display triumphantly on a platter surrounded by beautifully roasted vegetables. This little sucker is sad and somewhat pallid, but it's useful for many of your save-it-forward dishes!

The spices in this recipe will result in a delicious but fairly standard cooked chicken. Feel free to adjust them to fit the dish you'll be making. Cumin, Italian seasoning, and Cajun seasoning are great options.

1. Remove the bag of mysterious parts from the chicken (it's up to you where they go from here), and pat the chicken dry with paper towels. Combine the paprika, garlic powder, onion powder, salt, and pepper in a small bowl. Rub the mixture all over the chicken and sprinkle some inside the cavity as well.

2. Spray the crock of a slow cooker with cooking spray. Place the carrots and onion wedges in the crock. (The primary purpose of the vegetables is to lift the chicken out of its own fat. They do add a bit of flavor as well, but if you are out of veggies, just make a ring of wadded-up aluminum foil as an ersatz rack and place the chicken on top of it.)

3. Cover and cook the chicken on high for 3 to 4 hours or on low for 7 to 8 hours, until an instant-read thermometer inserted at the thickest part of the thigh reads 165°F or higher. (But I generally just cut into the thigh area and make sure the juices are clear instead of digging through my drawers to find a thermometer.)

4. Let the chicken cool, then pull off the meat and use it in your recipes. Store in the refrigerator for up to 4 days or stick it in the freezer for later use.

INDISPENSABLE MEXICAN CHICKEN

2 packages cheesy taco seasoning (don't judge until you've tried it!)

Two 14.5-ounce cans diced tomatoes with green chiles (Ro-Tel brand or generic)

3 pounds chicken tenderloins or boneless skinless chicken breasts

This is a go-to recipe for me, and although it's embarrassingly easy, I've served it to guests many times (and they invariably ask for the recipe!). It makes the base for a couple of dishes in Effortless Party Week (page 105), but this chicken is also a favorite stand-alone ingredient in tacos, quesadillas, or nachos—so versatile! I generally cook three pounds of chicken at a time and use it that week for a couple of dinners and a lunch salad. I will still typically have enough to freeze to pull out for a quick meal when I haven't planned anything (yes, that happens to me, too!).

1. Mix the taco seasoning and tomatoes in the crock of a slow cooker or in an Instant Pot. Add the chicken and toss it in the tomato mixture to coat.

2. If using a slow cooker, cook for 6 to 8 hours on low or 4 to 5 hours on high. If using an Instant Pot, cook on high pressure for 10 minutes for breasts, 6 minutes for tenderloins. Let the pressure naturally release for 10 minutes, then manually release the rest of the pressure.

3. Shred the meat with two forks, or if you want to be speedy, use a hand mixer set on medium just until the chicken separates into pieces of the desired size.

4. Let the chicken cool, then pull off the meat and use it in your recipes. Store in the refrigerator for up to 4 days or stick it in the freezer for later use.

OVERNIGHT CHICKEN BROTH

Chicken carcass from
a demolished chicken,
including the seasoned
skin

2 carrots, unpeeled

2 celery stalks

1 onion, unpeeled,
quartered

1 parsnip, unpeeled (trust
me on this!)

10 or so peppercorns

2 teaspoons table salt
(likely more; taste the
broth periodically)

Additional seasonings of
your choice, mirroring the
seasonings you used when
you cooked the chicken

Making broth is one of the great joys of my life—truly! If you gain one thing from this book, I hope it's the habit of making your own broth. You'll feel like a legit cook, and using homemade broth is so economical and healthy. If you use your slow cooker, you can let the broth cook overnight. Strain it in the morning (after a cup of coffee, of course), then refrigerate it during the day, and it will be ready for soup-making by evening.

You might be tempted to skip the parsnip, but please don't—it will give your broth a wonderfully distinctive character.

MAKES 12 CUPS OR MORE, DEPENDING ON THE SIZE OF YOUR SLOW COOKER

1. Place all the ingredients in the crock of a slow cooker and add water to nearly the top of the crock. Cover and cook on low overnight, or for at least 8 hours.

2. Strain the broth by using a large strainer and an even larger bowl. There's less chance of a brothy mess if you put the bowl in the sink. I have an enormous stainless-steel mixing bowl that works well; if you use a bowl that's too small, the broth will splash out.

3. Transfer the strained broth into a container that will fit in your fridge and cover it. Refrigerate until you need the broth, but at least until the fat rises to the top. You can keep the fat (schmaltz) for use in other dishes, but I generally just skim and toss it.

EVERYDAY VINAIGRETTE

6 tablespoons olive oil

2 tablespoons freshly squeezed lemon juice or red or white wine vinegar

1 garlic clove, minced

1 teaspoon Dijon mustard

⅓ teaspoon honey or sweetener of your choice (optional)

½ teaspoon table salt

½ teaspoon ground black pepper

1 teaspoon dried herbs of your choice (optional)

In a large jar or medium bowl, combine the olive oil, lemon juice, garlic, Dijon, honey, salt, pepper, and herbs, if using, and whisk until emulsified. (I like to use a jar with a lid so I can shake and store the vinaigrette in the same container. If you have a nearly empty Dijon jar, just mix the dressing in that without measuring the Dijon.) This will keep for 2 or 3 weeks in the fridge. If the oil solidifies, just set the container out for a while and the oil should reliquefy. Shake again before use. Or if you're a hurry, just microwave the vinaigrette for about 15 seconds.

SIMPLE SLOW COOKER MARINARA

One 28-ounce can crushed tomatoes

One 8-ounce can tomato sauce

One 6-ounce can tomato paste

1 teaspoon dried basil

1 teaspoon Italian seasoning

1½ teaspoons table salt, plus more to taste

¼ teaspoon ground black pepper, plus more to taste

½ teaspoon onion powder

1 teaspoon minced garlic

½ teaspoon crushed red pepper flakes

1 tablespoon sugar

You'll likely have the ingredients for this sauce in the pantry already, which will allow you to throw it together in five minutes in the morning. Add cooked ground beef or Italian sausage if you want a heartier sauce, or serve it plain over pasta with a Parmesan sprinkling. The simplest of dinners!

1. In the crock of a slow cooker, combine the crushed tomatoes, tomato sauce, tomato paste, basil, Italian seasoning, salt, black pepper, onion powder, garlic, red pepper flakes, and sugar. Add ½ cup of water and stir to combine well. Cook on low for 6 or more hours or on high for 4 to 5 hours, until the flavors meld. Taste and adjust the seasonings.

2. If you have leftovers, this sauce freezes beautifully. I will occasionally freeze some of it in ice cube trays so I can pop a cube into a soup for just a touch of tomato flavoring.

MATT'S MARINADE (and MY VERSION)

¾ cup olive oil

⅓ cup Worcestershire sauce

3 tablespoons brown sugar

3 tablespoons Dijon mustard

2 pounds grilling meat of your choice, such as beef, pork, or chicken

Table salt and ground black pepper, to taste (see Note)

My oldest son is a wonderfully inventive cook, and until he writes his own cookbook, I'm going to snag all the recipes of his that I can!

This marinade will work for chicken or beef (I haven't tried pork, but it should work, too). It makes enough for two pounds of meat; if you're marinating only one pound of meat, you can save the extra marinade in the fridge for a good long time (or cut the recipe in half).

1. Combine the olive oil, Worcestershire, brown sugar, and Dijon in a resealable plastic bag and add the meat. Refrigerate for at least 1 hour and up to 24 hours. If you can periodically turn the bag over to move the marinade to all parts of the meat, all the better!

2. Cook the meat per your favorite grilling recipe.

NOTE: Matt does not add salt and pepper to the marinade; he thinks they give the meat a better flavor when used as a seasoning after the meat is cooked. I do whatever Matt tells me!

My Version

I came up with a tweak that I use for chicken, though Matt's simpler version is excellent for chicken, too. To one batch of Matt's Marinade, add ½ cup Greek yogurt, the juice of 1 large lemon, 1 tablespoon brown sugar (for a total of 4 tablespoons), and 2 teaspoons table salt.

HAMLIN'S WHITE SAUCE

½ cup very finely chopped or processed green olives or salad olives with pimientos

½ cup very finely chopped or processed yellow onion

2 cups mayonnaise (Duke's is best here!)

½ cup Litehouse blue cheese dressing

½ teaspoon garlic powder

⅓ to ¾ cup buttermilk, depending on the sauce's use

If you hail from Muskogee, Oklahoma, you'll already be a fan of this sauce, which is really a multipurpose dip or dressing. It comes from the popular Hamlin's El Toro restaurant, and if you can believe the internet, this is the actual recipe. Oddly, it always comes with this sobering admonition: Do not put this is the blender. I don't know what dire fate might befall you, but consider yourself warned.

If you're watching calories, just use a drizzle on your Chipotle Chicken (page 58) to punch up the flavor, but if you don't care about such things, dip tortilla chips into this sauce with abandon.

In a bowl or mason jar, combine the olives, onion, mayonnaise, dressing, and garlic powder. Shake or mix well and refrigerate for 24 hours so the flavors come together. After this, add the buttermilk to your liking—less if you're making a dip and more if you're making a salad dressing.

CHIPOTLE CREAM SAUCE

1 cup Greek yogurt or sour cream (either one can be regular, nonfat, or low-fat)

1 chipotle chile in adobo sauce, plus more to taste

1 tablespoon adobo sauce, plus more to taste

A squirt of lime juice, plus more to taste (optional)

Pinch of table salt, plus more to taste

I have yet to find a Mexican dish that isn't better with a little drizzle of this simple sauce!

In a blender, combine the yogurt, chipotle, adobo sauce, lime juice, and salt. Blend until smooth and creamy. Taste and adjust the ingredients to your liking. If you like more heat, add a second chipotle. (To skip the blender, use 2 tablespoons of adobo sauce instead of the chipotle chile and shake the dressing in a mason jar.) Store the sauce covered in the refrigerator for 2 weeks.

PERUVIAN GREEN SAUCE

2 jalapeños, trimmed, seeded, and cut into large chunks

¼ cup crumbled cotija cheese (or grated Parmesan)

½ cup mayonnaise

3 garlic cloves

½ bunch fresh cilantro, stems removed

10 fresh mint leaves (see Note)

1 tablespoon freshly squeezed lime juice

1 to 2 tablespoons white vinegar (start with 1, then taste)

¼ teaspoon table salt

On a trip to Los Angeles, I stumbled upon a food truck selling Peruvian food, something that has not yet come to Pawhuska, Oklahoma. I can't remember the food underneath the green sauce because I was so dazzled by the sauce. Though I can't wholly re-create this dish because there is a shortage of Peruvian ingredients at Hometown Foods in Pawhuska, I think this recipe comes close. The sauce is incredibly wonderful when drizzled over Tex-Mex food, but I've also been spotted dipping my tortilla chips straight into it.

Place the jalapeños, cheese, mayonnaise, garlic, cilantro, mint, lime juice, vinegar, and salt in a blender or food processor and blend until smooth. Store the sauce covered in the refrigerator for 2 weeks.

NOTE ON MINT: Here's a handy life hack: I often buy a mint plant instead of a plastic container of mint sprigs from the produce aisle. I might not always get around to planting the darn thing (though sometimes I do!), but it yields about the same amount of leaves for about the same price, and surely a live plant must be fresher and healthier, wouldn't you think?

FROZEN FRUIT CUPS

One 14.5-ounce can apricots, cut into medium dice, with their juices

One 20-ounce can crushed pineapple, undrained

One 12-ounce can frozen orange juice, thawed

2 tablespoons freshly squeezed lemon juice

6 bananas, split lengthwise and roughly chopped

¼ cup sugar

Sprite or 7Up, for serving (optional)

I started making these for Christmas morning when my kids were little. They were premade and ready to eat, and I didn't miss one moment of Christmas morning fun. If you're serving them to a crowd, it's handy to put a batch in a large glass or plastic jar of a size that suits your family. Sometimes, if I have enough room in my freezer, I'll package them in single-serving portions, and I notice that my kids will (occasionally) turn to these instead of less healthy treats. If you're avoiding sugar, you can eliminate the additional sugar and add a bit of stevia to your individual serving, which is what I do.

1. In a large bowl, combine the apricots and juice, pineapple and juice, orange juice, lemon juice, bananas, sugar, and 2 cups of water.

2. Divide the mixture among freezer-safe and microwave-safe containers (in case you need to expedite the defrosting process before serving). Freeze until you're ready to use.

3. Pull individual servings out of the freezer an hour or so before serving so they start to soften. You may need to use your microwave's defrost setting to get them to the perfect slushiness, depending on when you took them out. My kids like to add a bit of Sprite to theirs right before they eat them (with a spoon), but I think they are perfectly sweet and slushy without it!

Acknowledgments

I am keenly aware that this book would never have happened without the incredible people God has placed in my life, namely:

John, the guy who would have preferred to eat meatloaf every week yet endured a life of culinary experiments: I didn't fully understand that I'd won the husband lottery when we got married thirty-five years ago, but I do now. Your unwavering, unqualified support is a gift, and I thank God for you.

My kids, who inspired this book: To Matthew, my firstborn—we needed you more than you needed us. It is awe-inspiring to watch you reach all your childhood dreams. To Meg, the joy of all our lives—your love and faith make us all better. To Patrick, the kid with a soft spot for Mama—I believe in you and your pursuit of your big dreams. To Phillip, the kid who is still at my table, testing my recipes— your music brings such beauty to our home. I'm excited (and sad!) for you to launch your talent into the world next year—are you sure you need to go to college? To Mallorie and Stephen—I thank God that my kids had the good judgment to marry you. Thank you for adding more joy (and new lives!) to our family.

Ree: Thank you for blazing a trail for me. Your weirdness delights me, and your goodness inspires me. You're my touchstone, Emma (the one movie quote I know).

Jeannine Bulleigh, illustrator extraordinaire: This book would be a mere shadow of itself without your talents. Every illustration is museum-worthy (even Ziploc bags!), and I'm still amazed that God brought you into my life through a Chamber of Commerce banquet. One of the highlights of this process was when you told me you overheard your daughter tell a friend, "My mom is an illustrator." Oh, yes, she is. I'd also like to thank your incredible sister, Carrie Barron, who was the first to take my unformed idea and create something original and beautiful. Your mama must be very proud of you two!

Brandi Cagwin, my recipe tester and friend: Your orderly mind, culinary skills, and dogged perseverance are a blessing to me. Thank you, Cagwin family, for the long months of the pandemic when you couldn't eat your own family's comfort food because you were eating mine! I appreciate your sacrifice.

Cassie Jones Morgan: I now know that it is a brave act to take on a new author, and I will be forever grateful that you took a chance on me. Oh, the questions you endured! Your coaching and wisdom were delivered with your signature grace and humor. Your fine mind formed all my formless ideas. You brought this book to life. Thank you.

The HarperCollins team—your unseen work has not been unnoticed by me. Jill Zimmerman, thank you for shepherding me through this process with such diligence, insight, and patience. Rachel Meyers and Janet McDonald, thank you for lending me your editing talents—this book is vastly improved because of your skill. Renata De Oliveira, your artistic talents enlivened this book. Lastly, a special thanks to Tavia Kowalchuk and Jamie Lescht—without your savvy and hustle, no one would know about my little book. Thank you all.

To the family and friends who are unnamed but in my heart: you have enlarged my soul. I thank God for you.

Lastly, thank you, God, for allowing me to help You gather families around the table. I am all Yours.

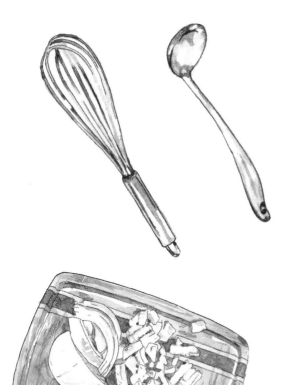

Universal Conversion Chart

OVEN TEMPERATURE EQUIVALENTS

250°F = 120°C
275°F = 135°C
300°F = 150°C
325°F = 160°C
350°F = 180°C
375°F = 190°C
400°F = 200°C
425°F = 220°C
450°F = 230°C
475°F = 240°C
500°F = 260°C

MEASUREMENT EQUIVALENTS

Measurements should always be level unless directed otherwise.

⅛ teaspoon = 0.5 mL

¼ teaspoon = 1 mL

½ teaspoon = 2 mL

1 teaspoon = 5 mL

1 tablespoon = 3 teaspoons = ½ fluid ounce = 15 mL

2 tablespoons = ⅛ cup = 1 fluid ounce = 30 mL

4 tablespoons = ¼ cup = 2 fluid ounces = 60 mL

5⅓ tablespoons = ⅓ cup = 3 fluid ounces = 80 mL

8 tablespoons = ½ cup = 4 fluid ounces = 120 mL

10⅔ tablespoons = ⅔ cup = 5 fluid ounces = 160 mL

12 tablespoons = ¾ cup = 6 fluid ounces = 180 mL

16 tablespoons = 1 cup = 8 fluid ounces = 240 mL

Index

SAVE-IT-FORWARD SUPPERS. Copyright © 2022 by House of Hyacinth, LLC. Foreword © 2022 by Ree Drummond. All rights reserved. Printed in the United States of America. No part of this book may be used or reproduced in any manner whatsoever without written permission except in the case of brief quotations embodied in critical articles and reviews. For information, address HarperCollins Publishers, 195 Broadway, New York, NY 10007.

HarperCollins books may be purchased for educational, business, or sales promotional use. For information, please email the Special Markets Department at SPsales@harpercollins.com.

FIRST EDITION

DESIGNED BY RENATA DE OLIVEIRA
ILLUSTRATIONS BY JEANNINE BULLEIGH

Library of Congress Cataloging-in-Publication Data

Names: Kane, Cyndi, author. | Bulleigh, Jeannine, illustrator.
Title: Save-it-forward suppers : a simple strategy to save time, money, and
  sanity / Cyndi Kane ; Illustrations by Jeannine Bulleigh.
Description: First edition. | New York, NY : William Morrow, [2021] |
  Includes index. | Summary: "Transform leftovers from each meal into a
  fresh new dish and put a home-cooked dinner on the table every night
  with 100-plus recipes and 15 easy weekly menus, in this first cookbook
  by Cyndi "Hyacinth" Kane, often seen on Ree Drummond's hit Food Network
  show and blog, The Pioneer Woman" Provided by publisher.
Identifiers: LCCN 2021041924 | ISBN 9780063042704 (print) | ISBN
  9780063042711 (digital edition)
Subjects: LCSH: Quick and easy cooking. | Make-ahead cooking. | LCGFT:
  Cookbooks.
Classification: LCC TX833.5 .K35 2021 | DDC 641.5/12—dc23/eng/20211020

LC record available at https://lccn.loc.gov/2021041924

ISBN 978-0-06-304270-4

22 23 24 25 26 LSC 10 9 8 7 6 5 4 3 2 1